A STRONGER HEART:

The Story Told in The Spirit

JOSEPH MCGEE

A Stronger Heart: The Story Told in The Spirit

ISBN: 979-8-3304-1117-7 (Paperback)

The views expressed in this book are solely those of the author and do not necessarily reflect the views of the publisher, and the publisher hereby disclaims any responsibility for them.

Paper Wrights, LLC
www.paperwrights.co

CONTENTS

Preface

I didn't set out to be a writer. My goals were to be a happy retired person living off what I had accumulated in my lifetime of work, to take nice vacations with my wife, to walk on beaches, to eat in nice restaurants, to enjoy pricey beverages. And I would go to church on Sundays, sing the old songs, say the old words, put money in the collection plate, wear nice ties, and shake hands with nice people. It was all established, a pattern, packed neatly in a box, sealed up and ready to be delivered. My life, my future. I didn't really know the Bible, but I believed those who were supposed to be leaders, they had the degrees, and they would dish up what I needed to know. I was fat, content, opinionated, and self-righteous. Just what they are looking for in the kingdom of Heaven.

A funny thing happened on my journey to the grave in my bougie little box. I got cancer, and the doctors couldn't cure it. It was not fair, my wife wasn't even retired and yet, all those nice vacays we thought about hadn't happened yet. Instead, like so many before me, my life was going to include long days in the chemo chair, vomiting when I get home, getting frail, unable to do much, and then they would hold a "celebration of life" at the stone building upon which my hopes had rested and put on forced smiles and whistle past the graveyard. Someone might ask the pastor if he thought I were one of the "elect."

Fortunately, God gave me another chance. Diagnosis and surgery were eight years ago, but after months sitting around being depressed and wondering what it was all worth, I was sent a vision in which I encountered Jesus Christ. Nothing can ever be the same after that. I still have cancer, but for the last six years I have lived a life of unbelievable adventure, discovery, and purpose. I am not the same person, my thoughts are not the same thoughts, my aspirations are to help others today, not for the "future" I had imagined.

God has put it in my heart to believe that you can have this kind of life also. A life where each day is a story unto itself; the past is irrelevant, and the future is never set. An eternal moment where meaning and purpose are joined inseparably with the very act of living and being led by the Spirit.

We do not need self-improvement books or yoga classes to be here. Those things are fine if you are led to them. However, all we need is full surrender to Jesus Christ, and a journey can begin on a path we do not know, our steps led by the Holy Spirit, being open to Him, allowing ourselves to be used as His instruments, listening, feeling, being in His presence. And trusting Him always, as He will provide.

There is no set formula, nowhere to send a donation, no rituals to practice, no place to go except wherever He leads. There is no rulebook to follow, assuming you know right from wrong.[1] There is no creed to memorize, no schedule to follow, we walk by faith, not by sight.

In this my third book I go through these things with extensive Bible references so that people will see that what I am saying is entirely Biblical, even if it's different from what they are used to. I take some liberties to explore the feelings of the real people in Genesis so that I can relate them meaningfully to modern people. But I never contradict what is stated explicitly in the Bible, and I show you that the things people assume about the Bible are not the only perspective from which to view it. For example, Genesis doesn't talk about how Eve might have felt about her experience, or what feelings might have led Cain to murder his brother. And it is perfectly legitimate to access those feelings from a modern perspective because I

---

1 What I mean is what Paul says in Romans 13, you who are led by the Spirit, who genuinely love God and other people, will never kill them, steal from them, lie to them, or entice them into sin. The ones who need rules to remind them not to do such things do not know God and have no connection to Christ or to the Holy Spirit. See Gal. 3:19. However, believers can get that deeper connection with a little effort and God's grace. "Ask, seek, knock." Christ is available as the Great High Priest, and He is waiting for each of us to come to Him in surrender with an open heart. He will do the rest.

have faith that tells me these were real people, just like us, not a fairy tale. And all real human beings have feelings.

This book is intended to demonstrate to you how you can have a better, more meaningful, and joy-filled life right now, even if you have cancer, or a sick spirit that makes you sometimes feel like killing yourself. You can do this even if you are currently just going through the motions of living a colorless life inside your own self-constructed box. It is meant to take you outside the box to a place where your cup runs over with peace, and where your inner joy supersedes the tough challenges that we must each face in this life.

My sincere hope is that this book gives you a perspective on Jesus that may have been overlooked or under-emphasized in traditional Christian education; one which unlocks the door to Christian spirituality, and which allows you to see what Paul was talking about in 1 Cor. 2:6-16; the deeper spiritual realities. Once opened, that door cannot be welded shut. And what is beyond is glorious.

For all the broken hearts.

"But whenever anyone turns to the Lord, the veil is taken away. Now the Lord is Spirit, and wherever the Spirit of the Lord is, there is freedom. And we, who with unveiled faces all reflect the Lord's glory, are being transformed into His likeness with ever increasing glory, which comes from the Lord, who is the Spirit." 2 Cor. 3:16-18.

Chapter One

THE MULBERRY TREE

Many years ago, I was a potter spinning lumps of earthy-smelling clay into vessels on a potter's wheel on the third floor of a repurposed tobacco warehouse in Lexington, Kentucky. Out back, just past the brick-strewn kiln yard were old L&N railroad tracks and next to them grew a great mulberry tree, the largest of its kind I ever saw. And, at a certain time of year, the great old tree would fill with mulberries so that the limbs bent and hung with ripe fruit. And then one day the children from the neighborhood would appear and ascend the tree until it was completely full of children ascending, descending, eating, and collecting the ripe berries.

The children were bright motion in the dappled sunlight, free from anyone directing or managing, and they shouted happily, teasing, laughing, joking, but helping one another—for they knew the tree had more berries than they could ever collect. Their peals of laughter filled the air from early morning till dusk. Then they were gone until the next year. One glorious day, a day of bright sun, a day of joy and no thoughts of any evil to dampen their spirits; and me working and listening to the music of their voices while I kneaded my clay.

What a beautiful metaphor for the Kingdom of God. Here we are, supposedly wise Christian people, fidgeting with our anxieties, hurrying to our jobs, worrying about our bills and the ridiculously high price of gasoline; and there is the memory of that day when the sun shone so brightly reflecting on the sweaty little bodies of an entire mulberry tree full of happy children.

To be sure, all this confusion in our world is a trick of the devil. People say "That's nice, but I must pay for this, I have to work, I have to get ahead. This is *reality*." The voice drops a full tone at the word reality, emphasizing its importance. But those children in the mulberry tree nearly half a century ago were also real, the tree was real, the old tobacco building was real, all of it was just as real as everything we have here today. It all existed in its time, just as we of the twenty-first century exist in ours. Sometimes we see what we choose to see. Old twentieth century people once thought we were modern and original, just as our children think they are.

Yesterday, I was on Scott Street in Covington, Kentucky on a similar brilliant sunny afternoon. It is early June. The sky was crystalline blue, with a few clouds that looked as perfect as if a painter had painted them. I had a cooler of drinks, and I was giving them out to homeless people wherever I found them. I stood with a couple friends chatting under a tree in the parking lot of the library and continued over to Seventh Street. And as we went about our excursion, the people we talked to were of every color, persuasion, and background. The common thread is that they are homeless, street people. But we saw no tears. They were all just hanging out in shady spots laughing and joking in the intermittent sunlight under the canopy of the trees.

My mind stretched back to when I was a kid, and we would walk the two miles from my house to Tacoma Pool in Dayton, Kentucky on days like this. I would have a towel and a dime. Given the hard choice, I would take the dime. For a dime, I could get a Payday bar and a small Coke around noon. We had season passes. Playing and swimming all day long we were taught that the proper defense against the sun was to burn, and then you would peel, and after that the sun would not hurt you. Going home, we had to run or hop across the hot asphalt crossing the streets. We were absolutely required to be home by dinner time. Scorched, blackened feet, smelling like chlorine, skin red and peeling, happy, exhausted, and hungry.

The homeless, mostly, do not care much about matters of race, or any of the things that separate us. There are exceptions. They are human, after all. But there is generally a spirit of living together and cooperating, out of necessity; and most of the time a positive vibe. The street, at its best, is like that mulberry tree. There is food, shelter, and life; you must know where to find them. People learn survival skills. Mostly, they help one another. They live for today, it being all there is really. "… each day has enough trouble of its own." Matthew 6:34. Yesterday and tomorrow exist for each of us as pictures in the mind, either of what could happen or of what did happen in the past and which we have no power to change. But today is happening and in this moment, we have power to choose our actions.

There is a laid-back kind of inner peace on days like this in the street. People hanging out (some with a pint in a brown paper bag), joking and telling stories. Quite a few of our homeless people have jobs, but the rest hang out in parks, on the street, or at bus stops, because they have no place else to go. See Matthew 20:1-7.

The street is old. I believe that if you were in Jerusalem two thousand years ago, it would be very similar on that street. Beggars, cripples and old men and men born blind, the sick, the lame, all referred to in the Gospels. And even Jesus, "For the son of man has no place to lay his head." Matthew 8:20. He walked those streets, healing, talking to people, announcing that the Kingdom of God is at hand. On the Sabbath He went to the temple and argued with the Pharisees, but the rest of the week, he taught the poor in the streets. And thousands of people would gather to listen, so He would feed them. Casually talking about the Spirit and the glorious things that had already come and having a snack with Jesus. Tell me brothers and sisters—wouldn't that be glorious?

Probably every town with streets ever built or that ever will be built is the same at street level. And the people of the street are the same. Overcome the language issue and they all understand. They share common knowledge. And the people there are eager to talk about Jesus, to feel His presence, to bathe in His light, or warm cold fingers from His touch. Do not doubt me; Jesus still walks these streets. Tears come to people's eyes when they hear His name. The harvest is ripe like those mulberries, and God's children are laughing on their way to pick and bring home all they can carry.

The street is life. It ebbs and flows as the tragicomedy of human existence plays out. Hot in the summer, cold in the winter, the poor are always with us. The strong and the weak, the wise and the foolish—they are as eternal as the street. But the rest of us suffer breakdowns over money, jobs, loves lost, fears of possibilities and dreams of time gone by.[2] We suffer anxiety and regret. We lose ourselves in petty issues of day-to-day living, while each glorious sunrise and sunset passes almost unnoticed. No giggle-ouch of toasted feet, no passing a bottle of RC Cola, no sharing a candy bar with two friends for lunch. No happy children stripping a mulberry tree of its ripe fruit.

But the street on these summer days is filled with shouts and peals of laughter, and people simply living. Like the mulberry tree.

[2] Not to say the street people don't have these problems as well. Most of the time, every life is full of both good things and bad. And street life is certainly no walk in the park.

Chapter Two

Eve's Story

The Bible tells a deeply personal story about Eve, but hardly anyone really reads it. Everyone thinks they know it. Everyone knows the gossip about Eve. Everyone knows the "official" version. But everyone focuses on Adam. Adam is the beginning of everything. Adam was the first. Eve is secondary and she was the one who Satan used to tempt Adam. Clearly, Eve wore the symbolic, non-existent pants. Adam, instead of manning up, said "the woman made me do it." Gen. 3:12.[3] What? We would have expected some manliness from the first man, wouldn't we? But no, first he tries to hide from God. Gen. 3:7-8. Then he throws his woman under the bus. It's all there in black and white in the Bible. Read it and tell me it isn't so.

Eve would have been physically perfect. And her physical eyes worked just fine, as did everything else. After all, she was the mother of the human race. And she and her man were naked, and they were not ashamed, just like every other creature God created. Gen. 2:25. And what was wrong with that? Nothing! After all, didn't God make them that way? And who is anyone to question God? The point is that Eve saw everything, and it did not cause any embarrassment whatsoever; and the same was true of Adam. They were as God made them. And they were comfortable in their own skins.

[3] Actual words were "...she gave me some fruit from the tree, and I ate it." Either way, it seems like her man threw her under the bus, doesn't it?

True, God admonished them not to eat the fruit of the "tree of the knowledge of good and evil."[4] This is the type of figure of speech used by people of long ago. If you think about it, though this is not any ordinary tree, nor is its fruit an ordinary fruit, like an apple or a fig or any other edible fruit. Jesus uses a similar device when He says, "Unless you eat the flesh and drink the blood of the son of man, you have no life in you." John 6:54. The spiritually blind couldn't understand Him then either, if you read the whole passage. Thus, we are talking about something spiritual, not merely outward physical eating and drinking. See Mark 7:17-23; Romans 14:17. "Knowledge" also can be interpreted as the loss of innocence and is sometimes a euphemism for physical intercourse. Genesis 4:1 KJV. And consider that "knowledge of good and evil" refers to the focus, or fuller involvement with and commitment to, the physical, non-spiritual world, as in to be a man of the world; to become worldly, to "know" the worldly existence in an experienced way. But the hazard lies in the fact that it becomes the focal point of the mind when we direct our limited attention to the physical, leaving the spirit to the side, because our limited brains are only able to truly engage one thing at a time. This is a critical fact, and a limitation of life in the flesh.

If you look at Gen. 2:17 and Ro. 8:13 side-by-side, both are talking about a form of spiritual death. And if you read 1 Cor. 2:14-16, you see just what happens. The passage is a description of spiritual blindness and the sight we receive through Christ.

This is also how the tempter fooled Eve, making her believe God wasn't truthful about the "die" part. (The devil used a *sophistry*[5] called a four-proposition syllogism, in this case using the same word—die—in two different intentions. God meant *spiritual* death and separation from Him;

[4] We also must, being intellectually honest, consider WHY God said they would "die." Worldly entanglement is the death of the *spiritual* nature—the flesh does just fine for its fourscore and seven with a worldly outlook. Ro. 8:5-8. Then it returns to the earth from which it was taken. It is the true nature, the spirit that withers. This answers the riddle in why God told them they would "die," and the serpent was correct is saying "you will not surely die." God was referring to the death of the *spirit* brought about by worldliness. Satan tricked Eve with a logical fallacy, introduced by using one word in two different intentions.

[5] Sophistry is a clever form of dishonesty, with words used in a disingenuous way to mislead and misdirect someone.

the other played a trick using the same word to mean physical death only.) We must be careful in life because the enemy is very clever with words.[6]

Before this fall from grace, Adam and Eve were innocent in the sense that they were aware of God and engaged fully with Him and were not merely acting in obedience to the obvious worldly wants of the flesh. See Romans 1:20. And that was the reason they did not know shame. See Gen. 2:25.

And it is clear that Adam and Eve had a close relationship with YHWH. He was present in their daily lives, "walking in the garden in the cool of the day." Gen. 3:8. And Adam and Eve, were made like Him and in His image. But as Jesus mentions in John 4:24, God is spirit. And so are we. See 2 Cor. 3:18. That is, God made us as spirits like Him, and *loaned* us bodies of flesh to live, work, serve and worship Him.

Imagine Eve, the beautiful, perfect, and spiritual daughter of God, made by the hand of YHWH, and living in a perfect garden, with a man to love her and attend to her. She is walking in her garden, enjoying the brilliant sunlight piercing through the canopy, feeling it on her skin, all warm and the breeze lightly scented with all the flowers God put there, thinking she was completely alone. And suddenly there is a handsome, devilish stranger talking to her.[7] She is completely unprepared for this—and where is Adam? The oaf is likely daydreaming or looking for a nice spot to take a nap under a tree somewhere. He certainly wasn't paying attention, or else why did he not intervene? And what happened, happened. It's not all her fault. Anyway, she introduced Adam to the same sinful desires she fell for, and he fell too, being completely unequipped to resist. He was just as guilty, even though he tried to talk his way out of it, as most men do.

What is obvious in this passage is that she encountered the tempter. And we must turn to Matthew 4:1-11 where Jesus was tempted with food when He was hungry, with testing God (pride), and with greed and lust for the things of the world. This last—the test of worldliness is the one we

[6] You might encounter someone on social media, in a book, or in person, who makes clever-sounding arguments for atheism. If you are not used to this sort of logical mind game, you would do well to ignore such stuff. If it bothers you, ask a minister or priest. Read 2 Tim. Ch. 2.

[7] Yes, I know for you literalists that the Bible says "serpent." Everything in Genesis has meanings within meanings. There is the outer, physical, with the snake and the apple and there is the inner conflict between the flesh and the spirit Paul talks about in Romans 8. The flesh wants to satisfy its physical desires while the mind needs desperately to maintain its ability to see through these things to the greater things of God. Therefore, to those who are willing to see outside the box, there is no inconsistency. And remember, the devil was once the most beautiful angel in Heaven until he rebelled, and God put him out. See Isaiah 14:12-17.

really need to consider. For, Christ was also a Spirit and worldliness is like spiritual kryptonite. It requires focus and concentration to dwell in the spirit, especially when it is tested. I have seen a student taking a big exam freeze up and sit with tears in her eyes, too frightened to even pick up her pencil. And many situations are like that. Better not judge them. The right circumstances and enough emotional pressure, and the same thing can happen to you. It takes training under duress to overcome our natural tendency. And here is where Eve failed the test because she had neither experience nor preparation for such a thing.

The devil tempted Eve to become mentally entangled in what is physical and worldly, losing sight of the spirit, because no one can focus very well on both simultaneously, and there are so many things in the physical world to grab our attention, especially now in this crazy twenty-first century, as you have undoubtedly noticed. Not only that, but there are also things that take up time and scream to be done first before you devote the first minute to God. Wash the dishes, take out the garbage, send the kids to school, walk the dog, pay the bills, clean the house, fix the dinner, pick up the kids, start the homework, and make yourself pretty before Adam comes home from the office. Writing this, I must remember that this description of life is very twentieth century. In this new century, Eve could be a doctor or a lawyer, and Adam could be the home maker. Or both may be breadwinners. Or the genders may be something else. Good grief!

Of course, we see "perfect" people who seem to be able to manage all this. But really that is just a perception. They often wind up on the psychiatrist couch, divorced, or worse. Nobody is perfect. And adaptation to one's role in a rapidly changing social milieu is complicated at best.

Certainly, the Bible was written in a simpler time. So, as the Bible says, their eyes were opened, and they saw that they were naked. Does this mean their physical eyes didn't work before? Utter nonsense. They physically saw the physical, but their mental focus and primary involvement was pure and spiritual. The devil's trick was the looking down, the re-focusing of the mind on the worldly, mental entanglement in everything but the spirit, and the result is the loss of the "sight" (intimate awareness) of the spirit and all things spiritual.[8] In John 3, Nicodemus, a learned Pharisee, was

8 See also Ro. 8:5-11; 1 Cor. 2:10-16.

Israel's[9] teacher.[10] But he was unable to grasp the meaning of being "born again." How can this be when the Pharisees had to memorize the entire Old Testament? Nicodemus was educated, but he was not spiritual in this sense. And this made him dull. See 2 Corinthians 3:14-16. And again, in John 9, the story of the man born blind, we see that the Pharisees and the priests were "blind" to the spirit. See John 9:39-41.

This story also teaches us something about shame. Looking at Genesis 2:25, 3:7 and 3:10, the verbs "were" and "was" are forms of the verb "to be." "They *were* naked, and they *were* not ashamed." Gen. 2:25. "...their eyes *were* opened, and they saw that they *were* naked..." Gen. 3:7. "...I was afraid *because I was naked...*" Gen. 3:10 (emphasis added).

No place does it say they felt guilty or feared God's wrath or that their first concern was disobedience or sin. Read the passage over. Guilt over sin and fear of punishment do not occur until later. It was not their initial reaction. What is their first reaction? *They made coverings for themselves, demonstrating that they were ashamed to be seen naked.*

They were afraid *because* they were naked. What's wrong with that? All the creatures God made were naked. They were perfect, beautiful. But they were flesh, of the world, made from the stuff of the earth, fed from earth; the flesh is a form of earth, really. We return it to the earth. That which separates it from earth is the spirit, and to become worldly (that is, consumed by the world; a slave to the flesh) is *spiritual death.*[11] See Romans 8:3-16. Those who have their mind (focus) on the flesh (sinful nature) will die with the flesh; but those whose minds are focused or set on the spirit will live. See Romans 8:5-6.

So, having re-focused on worldly entanglements, or as Paul says, "the sinful nature," or "the flesh," Eve has lost sight of the spiritual world and became too involved with the physical world and all its confusion to the point that she could not see spiritually, and then one doesn't have time to immerse herself in reflection and meditation to regain her spiritual presence

[9] Isn't it interesting that the name "Israel" comes from the words meaning to wrestle with God? We push the mind to the limit. And then go a little farther, beyond mind, and into spiritual contemplation led by the Holy Spirit. There is no doubt that Jacob was taken by the Holy Spirit in a portent of things to come and left with the limp as a sign that the spiritual realm is real. Gen. 32:22-32.

[10] The Pharisees had to memorize the entire Old Testament and recite from it on Sabbath days. They taught it to the people.

[11] The spirit does not cease to exist, which is the reason we can be saved, or rather, it is the reason there is something to save. But we become separated from it, spiritually unconscious, and blind to it.

with YHWH. She has been deceived and the deception, as Paul points out in Romans 8, is death. Death first of the spiritual life, so essential to living a full and healthy life as well as to salvation, and then death of the physical body. Life becomes about food and maybe this is the reason people became obsessed with toilet paper during the pandemic of 2020, when all the store shelves were empty, and you couldn't get it anywhere. They didn't run first to their churches in the stone buildings, first they ran to Walmart to fill up the pickup truck with what they thought was most necessary.

If you turned first to God, and then to helping your neighbor and understood no one ever died for want of toilet paper; if you were quick to think we were being tested and God was still in control, then you are probably a spiritual person. If you thought God will provide, there is no reason to panic, this is the reaction of a spiritual person. But apparently most Americans were not there.

And it is this, the focus on the physical and worldly concerns that causes us to feel shame. The "to be" language in Genesis does not direct us to misbehavior, or to violation of a rule, not even to God's commandment. Shame is a negative perception of what one *is* (sinful *nature*). A person can change her behavior, but she cannot on her own change what she *is*. The passage is not about mere obedience, but about the spiritual death and the worldly thinking that is the essence of all sin if you really think about it. Even David, the great king fell prey to worldly temptation. See 2 Samuel, chapter 11.[12] And when we read the Bible focused only on the worldly aspects of things; or like a cookbook, following the rules, we lose the deeper meanings. See 1 Cor. 2:12-16. This kind of thinking is the reason the Pharisees were spiritually blind. See 2 Cor. 3:14-16. They saw everything in terms of the rituals and customs of the ancient Hebrews; the letters in the stone, not in terms of a spiritual connection with the One whose finger wrote the letters.

> "Do this, do that, rules for this, rules for that, a little here, a little there." Isaiah 28:10.

[12] David knew the rules in the Law of Moses, but as in the song Halleluia, by Leonard Cohen says, "her beauty and the moonlight overthrew ya." A poetic way to describe the fact that we humans just cannot always overcome the more powerful urges of the flesh, no matter our intentions.

Consider at the beginning of Mark's Gospel, the reason people were so eager to go out and be immersed in water by John the Baptist? See Mark 1:4-5. They had made the sacrifices and observed all the Sabbath days, so they were ceremonially clean, but they did not feel inwardly clean, and this is explained in Heb. 9:11-14. The sprinkling of blood and ritual washings only clean us on the outside;[13] they cannot cleanse the conscience or forgive us for the actions that lead to death of the soul.

Therefore, Christ, the Redeemer, is essential to the justification of fallen human beings. For those who surrender to Him, He restores us to spiritual life and sets us right in the eyes of God. The spirit has the possibility to live forever. The physical body we have does not. We must surrender it to the One who loaned it to us after a brief stay here. A lot of people focus on the Rapture to escape thinking about the reality of physical death, which they are afraid of. Peter and Paul embraced physical death as a release of the spirit to be with our Jesus. The end times Rapture has its place, but we are told to take up our crosses and follow in the footsteps of Jesus, up to the place of the skull, up to the place where the Romans kill people they don't like. A symbol of more than death, of complete humiliation and full submission to the Pax Romana, the Roman peace.

I want to make this clear. No, I don't walk on water, nor am I immune to pain and fear. But my *mind* is set on accepting these things as the inevitable result of living in the flesh in a world created by a God whom I trust. I refuse to let anticipation of pain, fear and humiliation stop me. I refuse to yield an inch to pictures in my head of possible negative outcomes. Or to cancer and all the possible unpleasant things that might happen in the future with that. And I am determined to remain positive and happy in the blessings of the Lord to the end, with His help. To serve others no matter what happens to my body while such is physically possible, for as long as He lets me. I want to sacrifice to do so, whatever I feel is demanded[14], and if I can, a little more. I want to offer myself as a sacrifice for the one who offered himself as a sacrifice for me. See Romans 12:1. And I am not in any way unique. You can do likewise; it is a decision you make, not any special talent you are born with. If you make up your mind to live without

[13] It is clear that Paul is talking about the spiritual, a cleansing that transcends the material world.

[14] Or discern.

reservation for Him, you can, for as long as there is breath in your body. This is where we become passionate followers, not just armchair believers.

"...fan into flame the gift of God..." 2 Tim. 1:6, in part.

Passion[15] makes it possible to live a fulfilling existence in almost any circumstance. Like Corrie Ten Boom, Martin Luther King, and others, so on fire for their calling that pain, death, and persecution take a back seat in the mind, the will of God leaving no place for negatives most of the time. We still suffer, but we see it as a test, not the be all and end all.

But as Paul and Jesus and others tell us plainly, the spirit is eternal; the flesh counts for nothing. It is a tent, a vessel made of clay. So, Eve's story can have one of two endings. She can accept the way of the cross—she will probably do this better than Adam ever could because women all do this to an extent[16] in bringing children into the world—or she can remain lost as Satan, her seducer, left her, walking her walk of shame, sour and disappointed. And Adam, poor fellow, will probably just tag along. She is the strong one.

[15] Defined as an intense feeling of conviction or belief. A passionate belief is one that is dominant in one's mind and life.

[16] I was at bedside through the births of my children. My wife had considerable pain. There was a lot of blood and a genuine risk of death. She was very brave. The rebirth of the spirit can also be quite painful. My wife compares it to walking through fire. While most women have babies, few people, male or female walk through the fire of deep self-discovery.

Chapter Three

WHY DID JESUS HAVE TO DIE?

A reader on my blog page asked me this question recently. The short answers people give are "because that was God's plan," or "because it was God's will." While those things are true, we know God is merciful and would not sacrifice Jesus, His beloved Son, unless there was no other way to save human beings from their folly. Read Matthew 26:36-39. Knowing what was coming, Jesus begged the Father for another way. So, why was there no other way?

Earlier, we discussed the temptation of Eve in the garden, and the allegorical seduction that occurred diverting her from her spiritual life to worldliness, and slavery to the natural existence (flesh).[17] And we saw how this seemingly almost innocuous moment brought shame, the negative perception of oneself, into the world. A fair reading of Genesis 2:25 through 3:10 shows clearly that this is not just about following God's commands; rather it is about spirituality, sight, and our *relationship* with God. Paul understood this.[18]

[17] Some Bibles translate as "sinful nature;" others say "flesh." This is referring to what Paul recognized as the constant wants of the physical body and the mind continually bombarded by desirable things in the physical world through the five senses. See Romans Ch. 8.

[18] Paul writes extensively about spirituality in 1 Cor. 2; 2 Cor. 3, and the entire book of Hebrews, as well as other places. Jesus also talks about the importance of a spiritual understanding, and this is very apparent in the book of John, especially chapters 3, 4, and 9.

But intertwined with shame is *desire*, the wanting of the flesh, its yearning for all the things of this world with which it shares the nature of its physical existence. And when this wanting and yearning enters the mind, and the thoughts, it becomes idolatry, the lusting after flesh, the craving of the stomach, the wandering eye, the envious and jealous heart. All born of the wants of the flesh for all things of the world, of wonders and splendors and beauty, which enters our thoughts and dreams, and, when we do not get what the flesh wants, leads to scheming and aggression. And this is sin, and sin gives rise to theft, rape, murder, lies, adultery, and greed of every sort—selfish, profane, evil, low, despicable, and cruel.

"The wrath of God is being revealed from heaven against all the godlessness and wickedness of men who suppressed the truth by their wickedness. Since what may be known about God is plain to them because God has made it plain to them. For since the creation of the world God's invisible qualities—his eternal power and divine nature—has been clearly seen, being understood from what has been made, so that men are without excuse.

"For although they knew God, they neither glorified him as God nor gave thanks to him, but their thinking became futile, and their foolish hearts were darkened. Although they claimed to be wise, they became fools and exchanged the glory of the immortal God for images made to look like mortal man and birds and animals and reptiles.

"Therefore, God gave them over in the sinful desires of their hearts to sexual impurity for the degrading of their bodies with one another. They exchanged the truth of God for a lie and worshiped and served created things rather than the creator—who is forever praised. Amen.

***

"Furthermore, since they did not think it worthwhile to retain the knowledge of God, he gave them over to a depraved mind, to do what ought not to be done. They became filled with every kind of wickedness, evil, greed and depravity. They are full of envy, murder, strife, deceit, and malice. They are gossips, slanderers, God haters, insolent, arrogant and boastful; They invent ways of doing evil; they disobey their parents; They are senseless, faithless, heartless, ruthless. Although they know God's righteous decree that those who do such things deserve death, they not only continue to do these very things but also approve of those who practice them." Romans 1:18-30, in part.

You see, what has happened is that people have been diverted in their attention and in their interests away from the Spirit to the worldly and the physical and those things that are made from the earth, and away from God who is spirit. In this, man has lost spiritual sight and the ability to connect with God. And this is where sin comes from—greed, anger, lust and all these negatives that are born of the material, the flesh.

Man has in effect sold the spirit cheaply, exchanging it for things that are worthless and dross and rags instead of that which is gold and silver and precious stones. Spirit is much more precious than anything in this world, even our own physical existence, which is temporary. In fact, the things that have been created in the physical world are nothing compared to the things in the spiritual realm which are eternal and glorious beyond comprehension.

And we can perceive some of that spiritual realm not only after we die in the flesh; we are able to experience some of its glory here and now, at least in a small part. When we are obedient and following God and listening to God and the Holy Spirit is flowing through us like streams of living water (see John 7:37-8) we can feel timeless, connected, and eternal. We can walk by faith and not by sight. We can feel the Holy Spirit inside us, the joy it brings, and with God's help, we can experience that now in the physical world. Not all the time, not every minute of every day, but God does send the Holy Spirit to help us as we are obedient and as we follow him. And that is part of the reason the enemy, who threw away this gift out of arrogance, hates us. See Isaiah 14:12-20, The Morning Star.[19]

Back to Jesus. Jesus was offered everything, the whole world and everything in it, absolute power eternally in the physical realm, to sell out the spirit (worship the devil, practice the idolatry of power and possession) in Matthew 4:1-11, when he was tempted in the wilderness. Every man would be his slave, every woman his concubine, every material thing his,

---

[19] Lucifer translated means the Morning Star. In our understanding, this means the devil. There are modern scholars who debate whether there is such a thing as a fallen angel, or the meaning of this in Isaiah 14. We don't want to get lost in their debates. There is an evil presence, I believe a personality, that leads men astray, just as it did Eve. Whether you believe that or not you have to admit we are often surprised and shocked when some of our most respected people, like David in the Bible, are seduced by evil and do shocking things to cover up their sin. Only Christ was able to defeat all the devil's attempts. He is the true light of the world.

all the land his property, all the oceans his. He could have had all the kingdoms of the world, all the gold, all the jewels, all the food, all the women, anything, and everything he wanted forever and ever. See Matthew 4:1-11. Because he was the Son of God, it was all His from the beginning. (See Galatians 3:15-16[20]). But the flesh God loaned Him was the thing that wanted it; that would enable Him to enjoy it, to revel in it. However, the spirit is not like the flesh; it does not work on power, but on love and sacrifice; not on coercion but on giving freely and selflessly. Although He was the heir to God, the consummation of that physical gratification required Him to be flesh and blood. This is what He sacrificed according to the will of God. And the world in which His kingdom will be completed is realized in the last chapter of history, described in Revelations. It is not about pleasing the flesh, but it is Godly in every way.

Christ passed the test. He chose to die on the cross, hands and feet spiked to the rough wood with crude iron nails driven through the wrists and heel bones with a hammer. Hung up over the whole world in shame, naked. No comfort, no one taking his side; this is how he died. And he did it for us, for you and for me. In doing this, He showed us the way to exchange this temporary world of dross and ruin for what is spiritual and enduring and worthwhile and heavenly and permanent.

The sacrifice of Christ is the exact reversal of Eve's mistake in exchanging the spirit for the "flesh" in the garden. The symbolism of blood required in the Hebrew sacrifices, the blood on the doorframes in the Passover, and the final blood of Christ, who became a sin sacrifice for us all (See Ro. 5:6-8) shows the willingness of those who belong to the Spirit to take back the Spirit with God's help, exchanging the things Satan uses to tempt us and thus affirming our faith that only YHWH is true and valuable in all the universe. For the life of all flesh is in the blood. *This is one of the most important principles for those who see the Bible as one whole, the playing out of God's perfect plan.*

[20] Some say well, that made it easy for Him. But not so fast. They are thinking of the devil in simplistic terms. In fact, forget the devil for a moment. Think of a man, a human being, who has everything, wealth, power, good looks, popularity. And there are two angels, sitting one on each shoulder. And one says, "you promised to give it all up, not to even taste of it." And the other says "c'mon. One little taste won't hurt you." This is where humans fall and Christ triumphs.

In all of this we see the reason Yeshua (Jesus' name in Hebrew) had to die. I saw this recently as the local football team went to the Super Bowl. People in our modern age become more excited about football than about Jesus. They wear football jerseys and host parties and talk about football beside the water cooler or over coffee at work. They scream at the television watching a football game. Where is that passion for Jesus Christ who died for you? Would you scream for Jesus? Would you skip a football game in the playoffs for Jesus? If you did so, would you be unhappy because you missed an opportunity to watch football with your friends and drink beer? These questions are not frivolous! I know that many people think "if I go to church, if I tithe, if I serve on committees, if I help with a food drive or some other charitable activity, then I am covered." This describes me at one time, before I met Him.

Remember the story about Ananias and Sapphira from Acts 5:1-11? This story was always puzzling to me and a little scary. This story is included in the book of Acts to show us that halfhearted efforts and token gifts are not going to get anyone into the Kingdom of Heaven. In fact, they are an insult to God. This is analogous to those who promised their best firstborn male animal, without blemish, but offered a diseased goat instead. See Malachi 1:6-14. God expects our best. He gave us the best, the perfect, with no sin or defect, and Jesus Christ himself will judge the world. See John 5:22. He judges the heart. You can't fool him.

"For the word of God is living and active, sharper than any double-edged sword, it penetrates even to dividing soul and spirit, joints, and marrow; It judges the thoughts and attitudes of the heart. Nothing in all creation is hidden from God's sight. Everything is uncovered and laid bare before the eyes of him to whom we must give account." Hebrews 4:12-13. See also Revelation 3:14-21.

Therefore, Christ demands of us who call ourselves Christians that we have a *true* heart for Him. That we are more passionate about Him than we are about *anything* in the material world. Fortunately, if you are reading this it is not too late. God accepts latecomers, so long as they come with a true heart. See Matthew 20:1-16. And he puts them first. This is God's way. There is more rejoicing in heaven over one sinner saved than over all the righteous. Just like Scrooge on Christmas morning, we wake realizing that it is not too late; our hearts can be changed, and we *can* be the person Christ is calling. He will send the Holy Spirit to hold our hands and help us and he will never abandon us. This is the *good* news—all we must do is to take our first step to Christ with a true heart and He is there waiting for us where he's been waiting all along. He is the Great High Priest, and he always intercedes for us. But he doesn't accept lukewarm efforts, half efforts, or reserved efforts. He doesn't accept tokens. He wants us to be all in for him.

In working among the homeless, I have known many men who in their youth went far astray, some even did hard time in prison for crimes they committed in ignorance. Some did five, ten or even twenty-five years. I never ask about their crimes unless they volunteer information, but one can imagine. Some were in gangs and their bodies were covered with scars of bullet and knife wounds. Yet, many of these called the worst by society have now turned away from sinful lives and come to kneel at the foot of the cross with repentant hearts and Christ has accepted them! Sinners, are your sins worse than theirs? They have been unburdened of their guilt, as have I, and truly there is no reason you cannot as well, if you come to Him with honest repentance and submission, if you see your mistake of placing anything in the world above His Spirit, acknowledge your former blindness and foolishness, and live in the Spirit (by which I mean, "turn your life over to Christ") Jesus will say to you, "Your sins are forgiven." Matthew 9:1-8.

So, Jesus led by example. He reversed the devil's work on Eve by refusing the temptation to save Himself from the cross. He gave everything He had in this world to save a stranger like me. And you. He suffered extreme pain and torture, not because we deserved it, but because it was the only way to save us from our own foolishness, our pride, and our worldliness. And God raised Him from the dead because that was always God's plan. And in that, the devil's scheme failed, and the devil was defeated.

It would be nice if that were the end of things. But the devil is still around. He takes people bit by bit, working on them through tricks of the mind. He attacks them with shame and doubt. He tempts them with pretty things and with sex. He gets them drunk and high and seduces them. Then he threatens them with exposure and forces them to lie and steal to stay hidden.

There is a path to defeat the devil in all of this. But you must take up your cross and follow. It will hurt. There is no getting out of it. Where He led, we must follow. He is the Shepherd; we are the sheep, and we know the sound of His voice. See John 10:1-5.

We will also fail. Try and fail and try again. This is one hallmark of a Christian. We get knocked down by life, but we cling to Him, and we refuse to quit. We are not supermen; we have a super God. We struggle and even if we finish life in chains or suffer the death of martyrs for Christ, we persevere.

This is hard teaching, but it is also a hopeful teaching. Hopeful that every one of us always remember that we owe Christ absolutely *everything*. That we cannot put anything above Him or beside Him. That we cannot scorn the Holy Spirit which will come and help us and fill us up and give us the power to do God's will even when we are certain that we can't do it. No matter how scared we get. But the reward is as certain as the trial is difficult. We live and die in the sure knowledge that He is waiting for us to take us to a better place.

I hope that everyone reading this is encouraged and happy in the knowledge that today is like Scrooge's Christmas morning in Dickens' A Christmas Carol. It is a new day for you and me and there is no reason we can't show forth the glory of Christ in it. Today our cup surely is running over with *joy*, with peace, and with love in the Holy Spirit. Amen.

Chapter Four

Genesis Revisited

The first book of the Bible is very old. Parts of it may have existed as an oral history long before it was put in writing. Parts like the flood sound like they could have occurred long before they were written down and had most likely been passed by memorization as from the early times. Oral histories can be highly accurate, and this does not in any way suggest that anything in the Bible is unreliable. It is only in more recent times that people have concluded that things in writing are more reliable than the spoken word. But the ancient Hebrew tradition was that the "oral Torah" existed alongside the written Torah, was also given by God at Mount Sinai, and this is preserved today in written form in the Mishna and the Talmud. So, oral traditions are valuable and can be as accurate and as important as writings.

One reason this is important to know is that we do not have an original manuscript of *anything* written in the entire Bible, only copies of copies. Clearly, Adam never wrote anything. This world was created by God "in the beginning." Certainly, Genesis is among the oldest surviving intact books of historical significance in any culture or tradition in the world. Adam lived a very long time before Abraham, and Abraham lived and died 500 years before Moses, who according to tradition wrote it down. And despite what some people claim, my Bible does not say the entire story of the Creation was written at Mt. Sinai. Some churches teach this as if it were scripture, but it is not. In fact, God told Moses to write down the history of his travels in the desert *after* they left Mt. Sinai. The law, or written code, of Moses was written, either all, or perhaps just the Ten Commandments on the stone tablets. We cannot verify that because we do not have them, and no living person has ever seen them. We know about the tablets only through the Bible, and it does not clearly state that they contained the entire Torah, the entire law, or the Book of Genesis. The tablets and the Ark were lost when the Temple of Solomon was destroyed by Nebuchadnezzar.[21]

Another thing we may notice is that Genesis is spiritual in a way few other writings are. It is so much so that without an appreciation of the spiritual life one cannot understand it, and it seems like nonsense. See 1 Cor. 2:14-15. But when the spiritual eyes are opened, it makes sense, and it explains so much that is relevant today.

In chapter 18, three strangers come to visit Abraham. Then one turns out to be God in human form. And Abraham bargains with Him to prevent the destruction of the whole town of Sodom! In Gen. 32:22-32, Jacob wrestles with God! Clearly, these passages are spiritual and can only be understood by resort to spiritual discernment. To the Aristotelian mind they are nonsense. But we who have chosen to believe in the Bible and received the sight can see riches denied to the unspiritual people reading them. We "wrestle" with God when we go deep for understanding.

Man in his natural state was spiritual, connected, having a natural connection to God[22] and almost no earthly possessions. After the expulsion of Adam and Eve from Eden, they lived as free people on the face of the earth seeking food wherever they could find it. As near as we can tell the garden of Eden was in the Fertile Crescent on the banks of the great river Euphrates *just* as the Bible says. The Euphrates is in modern day Iraq. Food was plentiful with wild grains and fruit trees. After the expulsion of man from the garden, people settled into the nearby territory. The valley of the Tigris and the Euphrates is still fertile today, surrounded on both sides by desert.[23] Although the Garden of Eden is not physically present, despite various people looking for a physical place guarded by physical Seraphim,

[21] Rev. 11:19 mentions an ark, but scholars still debate whether this was the Ark constructed by Moses.

[22] See Romans 1:18-23.

[23] No, I am not going to get into the discussions about the Nephthalim, giants, "men of renown," where wives came from for the later sons of Adam and Eve, etc. Those are fun to talk about, but I can't see how these discussions will make your life better.

people cannot find it because it is hidden by God. But its memory is hardwired into each of us, which is the reason the metaphor of the mulberry tree struck such a chord with me. Perhaps you have something like that, some special place that rings true to you.

Everything in the Bible, especially in Genesis has multiple meanings. Doubt—disbelieving in the physical garden and all that happened there—is a result of being unable to understand spiritual truth. Think about the spiritual garden: a place where the spiritual man is not striving against man and woman is not in the pain of thinking her sons will die fighting, and sad that her daughters will be little more than slaves until they die in childbirth; things far more painful than the contractions of labor. These are the woes of real life, and Genesis teaches us the nature of the human condition; the matrix into which the sacrifice of Christ, the innocent Yeshua, was required to save us all from the miseries of slavery to the flesh.

But, after the seduction of Eve by the serpent, and the loss of full spiritual awareness, Eve and all her children are born into the physical realm, having only very limited spiritual sight and awareness of the spirit. And the allegorical seduction by the material world still predominates in people's lives. We seek the wants of the flesh, always hoping for something more, until we return to the dust, with little hope of relief other than drink and pleasure that relieves anxiety and pain for a mere moment, and then we return to the worldly existence where "life is tough, and then you die." So, the story of the worldly man is a tale of woe. Paul explains it very clearly in Romans 1:18-32. God made it plain to all people that He alone is the one who created heaven and earth and all that is in them; and the pursuit of everything else is futile as the flesh deteriorates with time. But people, in their wickedness fell for the same lie that the tempter, the devil, used to seduce our mother, Eve.

And so, we who live a natural life are dust, and to the dust we return. We eat by the sweat of our brow. We toil, we labor, we raise children and try to succeed in worldly life as best we can. Some try to leave something behind for those who come after. Many are broken by the cruelty of this world before they even reach adulthood. Our tears are a river leading to an ocean of sorrow. We spend our lives searching for the balm in Gilead, something that will take away the hurts of our broken hearts.

Into this land of sorrow Christ was born. There were no snowmen or Christmas trees or reindeer. Here He taught and here He suffered and died. But here God did the most amazing thing that has ever been done when He raised Jesus from the dead and demonstrated His power and sovereignty over all things; and the superiority of the Spirit was made manifest to all the world.

Chapter Five

EVE AND ADAM

"Everyone puts Adam first; it isn't fair. Not fair at all. Before, we had this wonderful dream life. Our Father gave us everything we wanted, and we ran around naked in the woods all day. We did as we pleased. OK, I wasn't perfect. I fell for a man with a smooth line and big teeth and slicked-back hair. One time, period. Who knew? I never met anybody like him before.

"Then Adam, Mr. self-righteous, throws me under the bus to the Big Guy. (mimicking voice) 'The woman made me do it.'

"The worm. He got his though. Work for a living. Actually, it might do him good. Grow a little spine. I have to stay cooped up in the hut with these brats all day. He's probably out right now having a few beers with those cave men he calls his friends."

You might be saying right now "Whoa, my Bible doesn't say that!"[24]

No, the Bible in this sense sticks to the high road. But we can imagine what life and marriage would have been like for two pampered and sheltered people raised in a beautiful garden paradise, and then kicked out into the real world. Can't we?

[24] The reason I am taking this liberty with the story is first, the Bible doesn't talk at all about Eve's feelings, but my faith says she was a real person, and every real person has feelings, and there are usually lessons in those, so I am explaining about our sinful nature through the eyes of an Eve who experienced life much like every woman to come after her. And while some of the details are imaginary, the explanation of sin in the world is not, and is entirely consistent with Paul's descriptions of the sinful nature. This literary device hopefully makes this material more digestible to twenty-first century people. We know right from wrong, but the devil uses every trick in the book to tempt us. The only one to successfully navigate all of them was Jesus Christ.

Or is it too much to ask? The church these days is so institutional it has lost its sense of humor. "Oh, Mr. McGee you're taking the Lord's name in vain!"

Really? Isn't it vain to have people polishing the same spots in the church pews week after week for twenty or fifty years and never telling them plainly what it's all about? "Be good and put your cash in the plate, we'll get you into heaven. Trust us."

Trust? The Bible puts it plain. Read the first three chapters of Romans. You can't trust anybody on this level except Jesus. Other people, even the pastor or priest, are all sinners just like you. Especially when you are their source of money. Read Mark; chapter 7. Look at the TV preacher with the slick hair and private airplane. I'm sure he will get you into heaven, right?

In the Bible, God only established one worldly priesthood and he also abolished it two thousand years ago. If anyone still reads the Bible, check out the parable of the tenants in Matthew 21. The priesthood (the tenants in the parable) were meant to be guardians and teachers to the Hebrew people *until* the arrival of the Messiah at the time God had selected for the salvation of the world. And the priests knew what Jesus meant. Matthew 21:46.[25]

We have one High Priest who intercedes with the Creator of the universe on our behalf, for those who know him. And that is the special function of a priest, which is more than a minister. The rest, those who belong to Jesus, perform the lesser functions of priesthood, like tending the flock, and spreading the word. Study the book of Hebrews and tell me I am wrong. It is laid out in black and white. No fancy speech. You do not have to read Old English or Paleo Hebrew. It is right there.

Anyway, is it any wonder Eve and Adam had at least one problem child? One who didn't listen; one who was never happy with what he got, no matter how hard he tried.

Cain caught the disease of worldly thinking from his parents. He was a glass-half-empty person. It wasn't enough that he had food, clothing, and shelter. He was bored with working in the fields and wanted more. But there was no more for him. If you investigate it, you will find out that a field hand was considered a very lowly occupation.

[25] Also read Hebrews chapter eight, verses one through thirteen. What is old and obsolete will disappear. And in 70 A.D. the Roman Legion destroyed the Second Temple, and the priesthood was completely disbanded. There could be no priests because they had to be consecrated in the temple. But God gave us a better priest, as you see in Hebrews chapter seven.

Cain's little brother got all the attention from day one. "Always pretending to be oh-so-grateful.[26] Always polite. Sickening. And of course, God is pleased with him. Mom and Pop are pleased. Everybody is so pleased and impressed with how disgustingly *good* he is. What about me? When do I get mine? It's not fair!" You can hear it now, echoing across the millennia. (God: "Sin is crouching at your door. You must master it." Gen. 4:6.)

Cain: "I'll master it alright! I'll show them! I'll show them all!" You could almost hear it in Dylan Klebold, one of the Columbine school shooters. Jealousy, rage, a sense of failure and shame, a belief that fate dealt him a bad hand. And this world will never be right for a person in this mindset. Half good, half bad, it is up to us to find the good and make a life in it with God's help. Without God, we tend to get focused on the negatives, and that is our weakness and the source of many of our personal problems.

The thing is, from a physical, world-centered perspective, life is *never* fair. No matter how rich you get, how strong, how accomplished at what you do, someone richer, stronger, or more accomplished always comes along eventually. And, all the attention, all the fawning obsequious phonies are gaga for the famous, the billionaires, the superstars—exactly the people who need it least. They are beautiful, they can do anything, they are always fabulous. Fabulous looks, fabulous clothes, entourages of wannabes, always shown on TV. And most of us cannot imagine what their lives are like, and think they are happy. However, the truth is that they are often the unhappiest people of all! Their divorces, rehab stories, depression and suicides are smeared across the tabloids like rancid butter on moldy bread.

They must stay on "top," they can't fail, they can't gain an ounce, they have tons of anxiety, they drink and pop pills to feel good, and they can't get rid of their phony friends or the paparazzi. And on "top" you are only as good as your "next." Next movie, next election, next appearance. Their lives are centered on what is false, what doesn't last, what is just a whiff of smoke in the end. And many destroy themselves with booze, drugs, depression, bad relationships, and suicide when they come to that realization. Ecclesiastes[27] had it right all those centuries ago. It all comes to nothing in the end except for God, the only thing that lasts.

[26] Of course, he really was grateful. He was good, through and through. But I'm describing how a bitter, unhappy brother might have felt.

[27] Tradition says written by Solomon.

And no matter what people do there will be suffering. These bodies of flesh were not meant to be permanent. Yes, look around, innocents die. People get by with murder. The world is a mess. And from all appearances it is getting worse by the minute. Of course, that is not the last word. God always has the last word. He is the creator and the ultimate power over the physical universe; He is sovereign over *everything*. This is where people get hung up about freewill and predestination. God always brings us to the point of reaching out; gives us the choice to either reach out or reach for the bottle, or whatever painkiller is our preferred poison.

> "The God who made the World and everything in it is Lord of heaven and earth and does not live in temples built by human hands. And he is not served by human hands as if he needed anything. Rather he himself gives all men life and breath and everything else. From one man he made every nation of men, that they should inherit the whole earth; and he marked out their appointed times in history and the appointed boundaries of their lands. God did this so that they would seek him and perhaps reach out for him and find him, though he is never far from each one of us. For in him we live and move and have our being. As some of your poets have said "we are his offspring." Acts 17: 24-28.

In other words, predestination[28] sets up the life situation for each of us, but still allows us the choice whether to reach out and find God; and there is an allowance for free will in making the ultimate choice. From Lucifer the rebellious angel (the prototypical narcissist) to you and me, the possibility always exists to make the wrong choice. Jesus, in Matthew 4:1-11, demonstrates for us how to make the right choice. And He was also tempted on the cross, when the Romans said, "If you are the son of God, save yourself!" Jesus passed the test but we who would follow him must be prepared to pay the cost. The cross is before us. We can pick it up and carry it or be dragged kicking and screaming to suffer and die, if that is God's will, at the hands of cruel men. But we received this mortal existence as

[28] Defined as God's will or plan.

a gift. We paid nothing for it. The flesh is temporary, it does not last. We make of this opportunity what we can with God's help.

The point of this whole discussion is to put out the message that there is a life here and now—today—that is still worth living, even when things aren't going the way we had planned, even when we are dying of cancer, even when our worlds are falling apart, when our friends desert us, when our children die, or when all the other catastrophes of life occur. That was the point of the story of Job, and Paul's point in telling Timothy we must bear our sufferings like soldiers. I looked at myself after realizing my cancer was incurable to modern medicine and I saw that I was still alive, that I was still able to do things, and have lived every day for several more years one day at a time, serving the Lord as best I can. Each day I remind myself, "this is the day the Lord has made." And the days have been worth living and I resolve to continue this way as long as He allows.

So where did this leave Eve? And all who inherited her plight? Exactly here: there is a choice. God is still available. He allowed Jesus, His only Son, to act out of pure love and compassion; to give Himself as a blood sacrifice to lead the way for us. We must take up our crosses and follow. Abraham passed the test, Moses passed the test, and Peter and Paul passed the test.

But it is not just a bed of roses. There are thorns. If you want to make the journey all the way to the end, you must accept things, give up things, and learn to be a "glass-half-full" person. Be grateful for what is given and let go of what is not given. And, crying over what is not given is not fruitful. Rejoice in the knowledge that we rest in his great gentle hands, and he will not drop us.

I do not believe the saying that God will never give us more than we can handle as some people say. I believe that God gives us things that only He can handle so that we will turn to Him for the ability to handle them. I believe this is the point. We pray for so-called bad things not to happen, but rather we should pray for the courage and strength to walk our walk when they inevitably do happen.

People put on a brave, but false face, when they get terminal cancer. No one, on his or her own, can "handle" it, that is, to persist in a state of inner joy in the knowledge that God is sovereign over all things and that He loves us. See Romans 5:3-5. For that, we need God's help. And when it gets scary God can give you courage beyond human capabilities. Human beings cannot withstand torture for very long. But God gave Richard Wurmbrand the ability to withstand the severest forms of physical torture for fourteen years. Everyone breaks under torture, but God doesn't break. I am certain God did this in Richard's case for our benefit who have been humbled because we know the story, and we know we could not do what he did.

Therefore, Eve *can* live a life to be envied, delighting in her living children, thrilled with the breath she draws, excited to be loved by her big, sweaty man at night. Or she can keep thinking she got a bad deal and feeling sorry for herself. Maybe she wants to make this change, but she needs a transformation, a different point of view or a different state of mind. How can she get there?

Chapter Six

Another Road for Our Heroine

This is exactly the point of what Christ says to Nicodemus in John 3:3. You must let the Spirit be born in you. Believe in Christ, and you receive eternal life. See John 5:24. The Greek word "zoe" used in John 5:24 for eternal life also means *spiritual* life. Something we can have *here* and *now* when we are saved. Notice it says in part "…whoever hears my words and believes in the one who sent me *has* eternal life…" John. 5:24. This is stated in present tense because it is available immediately, when we are born again in spirit. Therefore, God's gift of faith in Jesus is not just put off until after physical death; it is also a new life and spirit here and now. So, Eve is not condemned to always live in the miseries she has created for herself in her own mind. *She can have a spiritual life and existence that transforms her life into an experience worthy of the Garden of Eden right now.*

I testify that before surrendering myself to Him, I was unhappy. I was worried. I was anxious. Since that day, I have been happy most of the time. I have had very few days when I did not wake up happy and go to bed happy. I'm always happy when I am out doing my calling for the poor. I'm happy reading my Bible, writing, taking long walks or having a cup of coffee with my wife. I have been upset by losses of friends and relationships. But there are only a couple of times in over five years I have really not been happy, and they never last more than a day or two. Paul tells of a similar experience in 2 Timothy 1:15.

It is indisputable that we human beings have an innate sense of God's presence. See Romans 1:20. From the Native Americans to the Aboriginal people of the Australian Outback, and from the early cave dwellers to the peoples of India and China, the art, and artists of different cultures and surviving artifacts and rituals support this.

But man is so distractable, and so sensitive to chemical and hormonal shifts, that it is very hard to stay focused on anything, let alone on the spirit. Further, the mind is so active and imaginative that even if you still the flesh, the mind wanders this way and that. This is part of the reason some ancient cultures developed methods of meditation, but they did not seek God; rather they sought themselves instead.[29] And many people worshipped pieces of wood and stone and birds and animals and the creations rather than the Creator. See Romans 1:23. They instinctively knew that there is something greater than ourselves, but they were unable on their own to discern the full truth.

The pagan cultures of the Mediterranean area, well known to Paul, were very much given to the pursuits of the flesh. Therefore, God gave them over to their shameful lusts (Romans 1:24) and they exchanged the truth for a lie (Romans 1:25), and He let them abase themselves in all kinds of evil, allowing them to seek their own demise, because they knew what they did, (lying, killing, and stealing) were evil. See Romans 1: 26-30. But of course, He always had a plan to save those who will seek Him and serve Him. Thus, He sent Christ into the world to be the light in the darkness and to those who hear His voice. See Hebrews 4:6-10.

There is a caution here for twenty-first Century people. Religion is not the same thing as knowing the Risen Savior. I heard the word and tried as hard as I could with my very limited understanding. But even having the instruction, I sat for twenty years and listened to the sermons, singing the songs, reading the words. I was proud to be a contributor, a member, an elder. But that is not the flame of passion God wants. In fact, pride in

[29] There is nothing wrong with some introspection, it helps us to know ourselves. However, my "self" is a temporary existence. God is the beginning and the end of everything. The One we follow is selfless. He gave everything for God. We cannot even begin to follow Him unless we first seek God. And then it is a lifelong process, as we struggle with the flesh.

those things dims the light. See 2 Corinthians 3:14. Be careful! I had a partial picture, but no idea what to do with it. This is where the cancer and beginning the deep faith journey brought me—first to my knees, then deeper into faith, and into action which fed and grew the faith.[30]

He will challenge you, exhort you and let you suffer at times. My own deep faith journey is sometimes as painful as flames licking my heart and fearful as falling from a great height. But this is much to my benefit! It is the often-painful process of tearing down and building up again that characterizes the spiritual journey. Just as a caterpillar sheds its outer layer, and what is within is far more beautiful, and like the butterfly we can fly! Soaring on the wind, above all the flesh, the spirit we are destined to be reaches the heights that we might fulfill the purposes of the One who put us here in the first place. Thanks be to God!

> Whatever you have learned or received or heard from me, or seen in me, put into practice. And the God of Peace will be with you. Philippians 4:9.

Serving God in our lives and sacrificing our wants and plans, dreams and ambitions for God is the key to a growing and deepening faith, and closer relationship with God. Bringing canned food to a monthly food drive and putting money in the collection plate is the kindergarten-level commitment. Hearing His voice and putting one's own personal desires aside is the path to the greater depth and closer relationship with Him.

God has provided many opportunities to grow and strengthen faith by service. "Whoever tries to keep their life will lose it, and whoever loses their life will preserve it." Luke 17:33. What this means is we all physically die, and in many cases your faith, if it is weak, can desert you. If you want a faith that is strong enough to withstand an ultimate testing, you will have to *live* that faith. Like Corrie Ten Boom, Richard Wurmbrand, Martin Luther King, and others. Living the faith causes it to grow deeper and

[30] I have found out that for those who are saved, putting one's faith into action is an important way to grow the faith, feed the faith, and test the faith. Doing on a regular basis for others without expecting any return makes you stronger just as working out in a gym makes your muscles stronger if it is done regularly. This does not replace study, prayer, and meditation; it supplements them.

richer and more secure. (And also dispels much of our bad thinking like worry and regret.)

One of the traps people fall into is "salvation by works." Paul is very clear on this. You cannot work your way, earn your way, or buy your way, into the Kingdom of God; nor can one attain it by ritual, by sacrifice, nor by any outward sign. This was the error of the Hebrews. See Romans 9:30-33; Hebrews 4:1-3. We cannot attain it, we cannot grasp it, we cannot put it in a bottle and keep it. And we will never be fully complete until this life in the flesh comes to its completion. And every day we are put to new tests. First, being hurt by the people we love, and then inadvertently hurting those we love, which hurts even more. Wretched and tearful, because when we mean only good, we do what we do not mean to do! See Romans 7:15-25.

Not only that, but it is still so in the church today. People believe that baptism, communion, membership in a church organization, weekly attendance, confession of sins, giving money, prayer, singing songs or recitation of the Apostle's Creed will get them into their idea of heaven. And churches reinforce and support that. But while those things may have value for those who truly believe and turn their lives over to Christ, they are useless to anyone else. See Hebrews 4:2.

We must recognize that even the cruelest sufferings are tests that we must approach in light of the knowledge of our relationship with the Creator and with Jesus Christ. And the Holy Spirit will have to guide us through; we cannot do it alone. Guilt, shame, anxiety, and regret[31] are the whips and scourges of the devil and God lets him use them so that we will learn to let Him only be our salve for these hurts. Hopefully we learn to stop making the same mistakes, but we are certain to make completely new ones. Everything is in constant motion, and many distractions make focus difficult.

Life is hard in our world in the twenty-first century. We are bombarded on all sides with materialism, the dominant religion of this age, and most people just refuse to address this issue. Americans have fallen prey to the worst-case scenario. Desire of physical objects combined with access to personal advancement in society are the very types of temptations Jesus resisted in the desert in Matthew 4:1-11. However, each of us in the

[31] Remember, guilt is a negative emotion we feel when we have done something wrong, and we regret that; shame is a negative perception of what we are. We can change our behavior for the future, but only God can change what we are.

American middle class is faced with many of them today. This is the soft form of materialism. It is a seduction, not a rape, to use an analogy—it is born of the same kind of seduction as happened to Eve in the Garden of Eden. The eye is the window to the soul, and Eve's eyes were cast upon all the physical things she could have. Please tell me if you have never been tempted by anything the physical world has to offer. It happens to everyone. But only Jesus could resist them all. And so, we all experience the pull of things like food, nice things, and shiny objects. Glorifying our physical bodies is also a popular form of idolatry in this twenty-first century. That is why contemporary gyms have so many mirrors; fifty years ago, there were very few mirrors.

Two forms of idolatry are very prominent among church people. There is the idolatry of success; we are driven to win at all costs, and we teach our children to be "winners." This leads to extreme anxiety in some and even depression and suicide in a few. We cannot all be "winners" in the worldly sense. The other is the so-called prosperity gospel. This teaches that if we pray and believe, we will prosper in a worldly sense. This is very dangerous because Jesus Christ is not about prosperity. Read about the Laodiceans in Revelation Ch. 3. We should become enriched in spirit, not in worldly wealth by following Jesus.[32]

From our perspective there are important differences between worldly and spiritual mindsets. A person of deep faith is focused on God and guided by the Holy Spirit. This is primary and central to our belief. I did not do a risk benefit analysis or weigh the pros and cons before I went to volunteer for the homeless. I was led by the Spirit of God, and I simply obeyed. I did not plan, or even intend to become a writer or author. The spirit causes me to write and publish (at great expense) and I would be happy if sales of the books would at some future point cover the cost. If it were not for the cost of publishing books, I would be happy to give them away.

We do these things out of love, understanding that even if we are generous to a fault, and outwardly self-sacrificing, but out of impure motives, we accomplish nothing. See 1 Corinthians 13:3. It must be done out of love which is genuine. Reading 1 Corinthians 13:1-13, we

[32] I am not saying everyone should give away all they have and go about in rags like John the Baptist. What I am saying is we need to re-examine our values.

can see that an aspect or type of Christian love is what some would label compassion; but it is true compassion, not mere pity, and not to assuage feelings of guilt. We see others and we see ourselves in others, and we act accordingly as the "Golden Rule." *But the Golden Rule is not a rule at all so much as a way of seeing and living. Everything of value is heart driven and spirit led, and we walk by faith not by sight.*

Like Eve, we all have a choice. We can adopt the view that this is all there is and live to please ourselves or live to please other people. It all fails. We cannot do it successfully for very long. But we can also choose to acknowledge the spirit and the living God and devote ourselves to Him, let Him guide us and use us for the benefit of humankind. This will take our focus away from self and the misery a worldly mindset produces. Our hearts can be glad in the day, and in the joy we each share with our fellowman.

Chapter Seven

THE STREET

The street is the street. Always has been—always will be. From whenever human beings first settled into towns, to the streets of ancient Jerusalem, to old London town, to New York, to Chicago to Los Angeles, the city of fallen angels, and all the cities and towns in between.

In some ways, the street is timeless, because its parameters are those of life itself. People didn't ask to be born into this world nor do they recollect that. They are here, and the immediate challenges are those human beings have always had, keeping warm, keeping safe, finding food, and avoiding predators. We want our children to be warm, dry, and safe. Given these basics, a human being can survive almost anything.

Those who live on the streets of any city face the same problems as everyone else, the difference being immediacy. They have no stores of physical goods, and by the end of the month they are going hungry. Many of the homeless people have either a job or a monthly income, but it isn't enough to live on. Many are just people who have become displaced because of gentrification and rapidly rising rents.

We know there are predators in the jungle and there are also predators in the streets of every city in the world, and probably every city there ever was or ever will be. See Isaiah 1:21. And of course, if there are predators there must be victims. Homeless people may be hard to see unless you are looking for them. Often, they stay out of sight. They go off in the bushes to sleep, and many people only venture out into the open when it is daytime and there are people around and they feel safe. You might find them in bus stops, park shelters and other public places. You might not see them at all at night. But if you do, they may be sitting with all they own in a pile of trash bags in front of a gas station or the parking lot of a liquor store. They hope if they are attacked, someone will call 9-1-1.

Of course, some of the street people are addicted to things like methamphetamine, heroin, and fentanyl. They are largely controlled by those demons, and sometimes the demon is in complete control. It has taken that person over so completely that the real person who is afflicted is hard to see, and the spirit at times is almost completely absent from sight. Alcohol is another thing. Some people wake up in the morning shaking because it has been a few hours since their last drink. Despite the media hype, it kills more people every year than Fentanyl and Heroin combined. And the people who try to stop without medical detox often have seizures and wind up in the hospital.

The homeless street people addicted or not, essentially have what they can carry, and they are mobile by necessity. If the city politicians want to push them out of the park (sweeps) they go elsewhere. But like everyone, they must be somewhere. You can't just get rid of them. And they are American citizens for the most part, many are veterans, and many are elderly and disabled. Many have jobs; they pack and deliver your Amazon packages, work in your grocery stores, and serve you in restaurants. You never know it, but they do a lot of things for you.

Our society and just about every society ever founded throws away people, disowns the ones who don't fit some arbitrary mold. They do not just disappear. The widow, the orphan, the woman abused and left to raise babies alone, the father and the fatherless kids who either become criminals themselves or turn to drink or drugs to kill the pain. Others, the cripple, the schizophrenic, the rebel, the misfit.[33] And so, I readily see what is in the eyes of the street people and why many are emotionally needy. They're highly sensitive to unfair rejection and "othering," and to do-gooders who talk down to them.

[33] We have lost a number of our people this year. A lot of them were young. Some died of overdoses and some by suicide. Others died with chronic health problems for which they did not have access to adequate medical care.

To some people, the street is safer than the cloisters of the well-to-do. Here they don't get compared to people who have things most of them will probably never have. Really, no one needs these things, but they are often the armor of those who have them. They fend off the stinging arrows of shame that are thrown by the women of the ownership class. See Isaiah 3:16. This is the reason people feel such a need to have new cars and big houses. They fear the comparison with their neighbors. Some may feel a twinge of shame, leftover from Eve's misadventure so long ago. Why don't *I* have the latest, the greatest? What's wrong with me? This leads to envy and breaking the commandment. We work so hard to look "nice" and to have "nice" things. Why? What is the point? Someone else always has nicer. Are we any safer from the Reaper if we have a new luxury car or a million-dollar house? So, we lose coming and going. We cannot really win the competition of things; trying could land us in bankruptcy court. And in the end, we must leave them, never fully comprehending why they are worthless and wondering why we invested so much in acquiring them.

Society treats a man who hasn't had a shower or clean clothing for a couple of days as if he were "other;" or something alien, untouchable, disgusting. However, certain people would never accept him even if he were scrubbed, oiled, and dressed in an Italian-made suit and shoes.

You forget, don't you, that Jesus Christ was a homeless person. He and those who followed him walked from town to town and Jesus talked about a better way, something kinder for human beings, not dependent on laws or governments but coming out of a genuine love and human hearts. The only problem is that in this town that "*ain't*" going to happen.[34] And that's why the Pharisees thought that they had to kill him. He upset the powers that be, unsettled the status quo; and if you are really His, so will you. Take it to the bank. The politicians, lawyers, accountants, bankers, prosecutors, the councils of the wise, wealthy, and worldly will get rid of you, even if you are the president if you unsettle them too much. And unfortunately, so will the church. Their book of doctrines set in stone more rigid than the tablets of Moses, must be adhered to the letter, no thought or serious discussion allowed. These do not necessarily follow the words originally written in the

[34] In fact, many of our local governments are conducting a "crack down" against the homeless, even arresting them, breaking up their camps, stopping them on the street when they have done nothing wrong, and other cruel actions in a vain effort to get rid of them.

Bible, they are understandings of men, some written hundreds of years ago by priests or leaders as sightless as the Pharisees of Jesus' day. And modern commentaries based on the things said by men of learning hundreds of years ago triumph over the simple gospel as related by Paul who was appointed Apostle of Jesus Christ by the Grace of God. See 1 Cor.1:1; 1:20-25.[35]

Jerusalem was a theocracy, run by a council of priests called the Sanhedrin. The monarch, Herod, was mostly a figurehead. The Romans had conquered everything but didn't interfere with local government so long as taxes were paid and there was no trouble.[36] "Pax Romana" they called it. The Roman peace. Jesus got people excited; the Romans did not like excitement among the conquered people. They knew that in their vast empire, if people started to get excited, there would not be enough legions in all the world to keep them in order. And the Romans above all loved order. The Sanhedrin also liked a stable, orderly society because their position as the middlemen was secured by the power of Rome. They enforced their rules, collected their korban, Caesar collected his taxes, and nothing ever changed. Exactly what they wanted. But this was not God's plan.

You see, when God created the heavens and the earth, he already had a plan. And his plans are perfect. Our human plans—whatever they are—get swept up like chaff and thrown in the fire because God is ready to complete the bridal chamber, the Son of a carpenter is going to marry, and they are putting an extra wing on the house for the happy couple and their children.[37] This was *always* reserved for them, and the time was approaching for the nuptials. This is the wedding referenced in Matthew 22:1-11, the parable of the wedding feast. It is an analogy for the union of Christ and His true believers. The Levitical priesthood, the learned Pharisees, and the leaders of the Hebrews, were the invited guests who refused to attend. And so, the street was invited to fill the hall and take their places. Be advised however, anyone who has not surrendered to Him will be put out. This is the "wedding garment" lacked by one who was cast out in the parable. So, if you want to be part of the glorious feast, just surrender your life to Jesus

[35] Read Acts 13 to see exactly the gospel as Paul preached it.

[36] The Hebrew ruling council.

[37] This is the analogy of the Hebrew wedding in Jesus' day. The groom paid the father-in-law-to-be the bride price and then went home and built an addition onto the family home for them to live in. Only then could he come back and collect his bride.

today, and live for Him from now on. Cast off the worldly demands of the temporary bosses. You may wind up on the street, but they will wind up in the fire if they do not do likewise.

All these things did disrupt the streets of old Jerusalem a bit. Here came a poor man, a homeless beggar from Nazareth, the poorest part of the land, where everyone worked with their hands. He didn't come out of a great center of learning. Nazarenes spoke the common tongue. Son of a carpenter, His best friends were the sons of fishermen.[38] But he came healing lepers, making cripples walk and giving sight to the blind—and even raising the dead. The priesthood could do none of these things. Their robes and their incantations and ceremonies gave them no real power. Their rote recitations of the Torah on Sabbath days did not move them or their audiences. Their rituals were empty; their only "power" was political, worldly, the powers of money, of governments, and of swords.

And Jesus walked into the temple like he owned it and chased out the moneylenders and usurers, friends of the Priesthood and contributors. Then, he spoke a doctrine that the priests, being worldly, didn't comprehend,[39] and which threatened to disrupt the flow of money and unsettle the power structure, and he didn't keep the traditions and the statutes. He occasionally ate without washing, he worked on the Sabbath, he argued with the priests and the teachers of the law.

In response, the learned priests, and Pharisees, using the weapon they had, knowledge of scripture, followed him around in the street challenging him. This was a foolish political move because the incumbent does not challenge the contenders. This always amounts to an admission that the contender is serious, and that those in power fear him. And Jesus like a champion beat them at their own game flawlessly every time. And they could see that only through treachery could he be beaten; only by taking him at night in some out-of-the-way spot away from the crowd and trying him in a secret trial where the verdict was a forgone conclusion could they have grounds to demand the Romans execute him. And, for them to retain their power He had to die.

And of course, all of this was known by God from the foundations of the earth. So, when Abraham was obedient and God did not make him kill

[38] These were humble professions, did not require education, and people lived mostly hand to mouth.

[39] See John 3:1-15. Also see, John 9:39-41; 1 Cor. 2:14-16; 2 Cor. 3:14-15.

Isaac but instead substituted a ram whose horn was caught in a thicket at the last minute (Gen. 22:9-12), God showed that at the time of the fulfillment of his plan there would be a *substitute* sacrifice for the reconciliation of man, and the sacrifice of a son would be God's to make. It was enough to see that Abraham was fully obedient and willing to set himself aside for God. The incident was put into the scripture and recorded for all time though, as a pattern for God's plan. God seems to love to announce what He is going to do and watch and see if we "get" it. And here we can see, in the first book of the Bible, the outline of the gospel. God already knew what He was going to do, but we get to watch it play out with no spoilers.

To be clear, in talking about blood we are not saying God is bloodthirsty, or that He needs blood, or even desires blood or anything else from the material world. Blood is symbolic of life; and it has always been symbolic of a deeper commitment. That is the reason there are "blood brothers" and "blood oaths." The life of all flesh is in the blood. The Hebrew word for man is Adam. The Hebrew word for blood is "dam." God gives us our physical life, flesh, made from the earth. It belongs to God, and it is to be reclaimed by God each at his or her appointed time. And we are not just the flesh; we are spirit. When the flesh is gone, we are all equal. This is true whether we die as children or live to be one hundred years old. Viewed with worldly eyes, it makes no sense for children to suffer and die. But, for the spiritual it means that this served the bigger plan. And in the eternal realm the child takes up his golden crown just like others. He or she is not crippled or cognitively challenged in eternity. [This is so important to understand. You see a challenged person or a dead person in the temporary physical world. But in the eternal realm, he or she is a fully mature spirit, and at the resurrection, he or she will be raised fully perfected and whole.]

So, is it a surprise that Jesus came to us on the street? God sent his Son to us as a homeless street person. For every kingdom, nation, tribe, and empire of man is doomed to fall and be trampled into dust in time. But the street is still here—in Jerusalem, in London, in New York, China, India and Russia as well. The street is the street and will remain so until the last day. Ask any of the people who live there, the street is the street. It is what it is. And here in the street the Messiah came revealing good news to the people the world rejected.

> "But God chose the foolish things of the world to shame the wise; God chose the weak things of the world to shame the strong. God chose the lowly things of the world and the despised things—and the things that are not—to nullify the things that are so that no one may boast before him." 1 Corinthians 1: 27-29.

We human beings sin by making more of ourselves than we should. See Romans 12:3. We can't help it. This is a sin habit that is hard to break. Whether we are smart or strong, we think we are something because we are smart or strong. But if we are humble, we tend to think we are something because we are humble. If we suffer for Christ, we think we are something because we have suffered for Him. Hello! God has made billions of us, only a relative few will be saved. Not because God cannot accommodate them; but because they are just too stubborn and worldly to see.

That is one reason God chastises and makes His children suffer in this world. Only when we give up all that we think we are, do we become anything, including the idea that we are special because we are *trying* to become selfless. It is the ego, or self, that is the obstacle to living fully with God. But living flesh *cannot* become completely selfless. And therefore, I know the street remains what it is, and the people of the street who have been with us always, will remain with us until the Most High God, Creator of the universe, blows the whistle and the whole kit and caboodle comes crashing down around us and we are all standing before the risen Christ to be judged. See John 5:22-23. Even the dead will come out of their graves to be judged. See John 5:28-30. And as our beloved Paul, Apostle of Christ by the grace of God, says, "there [will be] no difference between male or female, slave or master, Jew, or gentile. For, we are all one in Christ." Gal. 3:26-29.

I can tell you growing up in the way I did, and then living in some of the places I lived, and working with homeless people for some years now, this is the way all creation is arranged. The homeless are not "perfect," but life is hard, a certain kind of cooperation makes it possible; people help one another. People—because of necessity—overlook race, gender, or background in order to live; and no one asks questions about the past.

Last night I was talking to a Christian man of the street. He likes my writing, and we talk often. He has taken to going to a place where homeless friends gather and talking about Jesus, telling a simple gospel. And yesterday a woman walked by and one of the men started commenting about her body. My friend explained to him that he was really belittling her and making her less-than. And the man was touched in his heart and repented. Later, a second woman walked by, and someone else made a lewd remark. The man who had repented called him on it and explained that this remark belittles women and makes them less-than. The second man then also was touched in his heart and repented. This is a true tale from the street told to me by a man of God. So, I pray:

"Mighty one of Israel: may the word of Christ spread in the streets from here to New York, from Los Angeles to San Francisco, and to China and India, and from London to Paris. May the sacred eternal street catch fire and spread like burning grass until the whole world is engulfed with a burning passion for you. May the wind drive it along and spread it from place to place on air filled with embers. May every street be a church and every alleyway a pulpit until all people are brought to repent of their worldly wickedness and kneel at the foot of the cross to be washed by the power of the blood. May killing and murder cease; may lust and envy see their end. May hate and revenge be rooted out like pus from a wound. May the fire of Christ Jesus cauterize the whole earth. Amen."

I must be honest though. The street is also the sewer of this world. Every form of cruelty is there. Addicts, thieves, the vicious, the terrible; shootings and rapes and people left to die in their own bodily fluids are all there. These things are also part of life on the street. People left hungry, people found frozen in parking structures, police sometimes sympathize, but often not. The street cops are underpaid and overworked, and the poor increase their workload. People get drunk and overdose and fall asleep in inconvenient places. There are fights and altercations the police must break up, and sometimes even murder. The police really don't like having to deal with those; who would? So, I do not have a "candy and unicorns" perception of the street. It is what it is. And some people are forced to live there; and some of them can be happy, with an inner joy and acceptance and gratitude for what they have despite these facts. But overall, this life is dirty, terrifying, and cold. And people are suffering and dying.

Chapter Eight

THE ECCLESIA

Before we can expect to light the world on fire though, we must light *ourselves* on fire. As I said, I have watched people as local sports teams have been in playoffs like football, baseball, and basketball, including March Madness, etc. They wear clothing with their team logos. They talk about the last game, the next game. Who is in, who is out? They scream at the television during play.

Does anyone come to work wearing Jesus' logo sweatshirts? Does anyone talk excitedly about salvation at the water cooler? Does anyone scream when Jesus has the winning point? I don't see it. Why not? Because only very few in the mainstream church organizations seem to be really excited about Jesus. They think going to church and putting money in the plate and occasionally helping some organized activity for the poor will get them into heaven, and they are bored. They are so used to doing what is required all the time. Football is an escape from the boredom of required activities. Church is more like a required activity, they know they "should" do better, but they are too tired from work, school, family, social obligations, house chores, bills, traffic, shopping, kids, etc. Why should any of that lukewarm stuff get you anywhere? They are like the people in Revelation 3:14-17.

I have been very hard on the institutional church in the past. But doesn't everyone bear some responsibility? Who complains when church activities conflict with sporting events? Who insists on being home on

Sunday before kickoff? Who places these things above Christ in priority? Who prioritizes family commitments over Christian gatherings or just does not have time to honor a calling from God? I can't claim any superiority. I used to do the same things myself.[40]

But the churches demand money, and do not consider gifts to the poor to be an adequate substitute. And most churches do not help the poor enough to justify their million-dollar budgets. Therefore, we are all guilty. We are all thieves, even though we are not aware of how we steal or of the lies we tell. See Romans 2:1-6. To change, we must get right with God first. We cannot do it on our own. It requires an inner *transformation*; not lip service, not going through the motions. Christ must be written on our hearts as if with a branding iron, indelible, permanent. See Jeremiah 31:27-34; 2 Cor. 5:17-19; Gal. 4:1-7.

I want to make clear that I am not talking about "conversion." You can convert from Baptist to Presbyterian or from Methodist to Catholic or vice versa. It makes no difference. I am talking about transformation of the mind and of the heart. This is so deep that we say the old person is "dead" and you are now a new person, born again of the spirit. You may be very little like the old you. You certainly will need to change your old ways and break bad habits, which is a lifelong process. But the Holy Spirit will be with you to help. Sometimes His help can be very painful. I wanted a deeper relationship with Christ, and I got it. I wanted to lose fears and anxieties I had from childhood, and I got that. The cost is that I have cancer, and so far, the doctors cannot cure it. I have accepted that but it's tough.

The transformation is real, but there is the cross. No way back, no way around. The only way out is through. There is pain, there are hard goodbyes, and things I must surrender. But victory is close. I used to think about the *idea* of Christ as just a salvation in the afterlife (pardon from hell), and the rewards of heaven were more hopes than belief. Really, the right question was the one asked by musician Jimi Hendrix in the 1960s:

[40] I cannot stress too much that I am not saying this to arouse guilt and shame, or anxiety. Jesus died to rid those who follow Him of these things; they are the devil's instruments. Nor can good deeds or alms or rituals get you into Heaven. 1 Cor. 13:3. Rather, we must open our spiritual eyes, open our hearts, open our minds to what is "outside the box." We need to get over the stumbling block that Nicodemus struggled with and the spiritual blindness of the Pharisees. When we stop "othering" people, seeing them as "less-than," and start learning to see the good in everyone, we can begin to walk Jesus' path. When we middle class Americans turn over our worldly lives fully to Him, we can begin to develop into the people He wants us to be.

"are you experienced[41]?" Well, are you? My own experience is unique but not dissimilar to things I have heard and read about. I wrote it down and published a book about it. I reprinted the chapter setting out my vision in some detail as an appendix in my second book. Part of it is not too dissimilar from the experience of salvation Richard Wurmbrand described in his book Tortured for Christ, or what the Samuel L. Jackson character described in the movie Sunset Limited, where he was in prison and God spoke to him. And people I know personally have testified to similar things. And certainly, while less elaborate than Scrooge's experience in A Christmas Carol, by Charles Dickens, it was along similar lines. And, like Scrooge on Christmas morning, I was blessed to realize that I was still alive, and it was not too late for me to experience the joy of living in the Holy Spirit here and now.

Unfortunately, I think most people either suppress these experiences or dismiss them or just keep them secret for fear of persecution, laughter, or scorn from those people who are being used by the devil. Nobody wants to be laughed at and scorned. See Matthew 5:11-12. And persecution can come from "good" people and even friends, as they are tricked, and above all the evil one is a trickster.

In the church that I attended for twenty years I never heard anyone confess stories of dramatic salvation experiences. They were very good at keeping things to themselves. But here is the big secret: Jesus Christ is real. He is present. He sees and hears you when you call on him in all sincerity. He showed himself to me and spoke to me in a powerful once-in-a-lifetime vision; And this is the experience I told. It is also the gospel; that is, the good news for you and me and everyone. I am certainly no better than anyone, just maybe luckier. Lucky to have received the word that saves and lucky the Holy Spirit has used me to pass it on and blessed to have been too broken and afraid to resist it or ignore it and blessed because the spirit brings inner joy and peace wherever it goes.

---

[41] Before anyone goes running off to their minister with their hair on fire, I am not advocating any sort of chemical enhancement as part of this experience. Millions of my generation tried this and it did not work. In fact, my recommendation is to not take any kind of drug, alcohol, nicotine, or anything else ever unless it becomes a medical necessity. The reason is that God, who created us already equipped us with everything we need to meet the Risen Lord. We have to scrape off the dross of this world, and He is waiting for us. Drugs and alcohol just get in the way.

Many of those who don't believe have been brainwashed. They can accept that The Big Bang "just happened" without asking why or what could have caused it.[42] They can believe a talking head on YouTube talking about something billions of years in the past or in the future and accept it as if it were a proven fact but can't believe there is a role for God in this. The public schools have pushed the doctrine of materialism until few are left who can perceive *anything* in the spirit.

The authorities of this fallen world have blinded people intentionally so that they can believe we can create a utopia built and managed by people who are broken and deluded by the desires of the flesh, worldly wants, physical beauty, shining objects, or sounds and lights and the feel-good brain chemicals aroused by drugs or by sexual activity. As I mentioned in *Twice Blessed: First Century Christians in a Twenty-First Century World*, this is a false premise.

It is impossible for human beings in their fallen state to create a perfect society. It is impossible for a human in his fallen state to do anything perfect. It is impossible for us to live together in a manner that is altogether peaceful and prosperous for everyone because the wants of the flesh pull us constantly; and because people are fickle, self-centered, unbalanced, and unreliable just as much as everything in this fallen world. It has been written about since Plato, tried since Moses, and it doesn't work because it can't work. Even the law of Moses, given by God with fire and thunder is unable to cleanse the conscience of man. See Hebrews 9:6-9. If the law given directly by God to Moses could not perfect humanity, how could anyone think that some law written by a broken, fallible human being will do so? Or that any scheme concocted in the halls of a bureaucratic government run by politicians and "partners of thieves" (See Isaiah 1:23) could perfect human society?

I have written about the fall and how Eve was lured by the wants of the flesh and became a worldly, unspiritual person and spread her worldly confusion to Adam. And since then, the entire human race has been bound in chains of worldly desire, which blinds us to the truth of the Spirit, and only a few even try to overcome it. It is because our brains are addicted to

[42] I realize that "the big bang" is controversial for many Christian believers. Others accept it as "science." I'm not taking sides. I'm merely pointing out that whichever side of the science-religion debate you are on some of these arguments are illogical.

the "feel good" chemicals our bodies produce; like endorphin, oxytocin, serotonin, and dopamine, which were intended to help us, but the devil used them to trick us and trap us.[43] And that is how we become slaves to sin. And the only way out of the slavery of sin is to recognize and turn our lives over to a "higher power." The wise recognize that the only genuine "higher power" is the God who created the heavens and the earth.

But many have been confused by the "god" of Sunday school and candy and Christmas, of Easter bunnies and Santa Claus. That is, the false god of presents and candy, teaching idolatry (desires of the flesh) to the young to their detriment. That "god" is fake, or at least is not a genuine description of the God who created the Universe and holds the fate of humankind in the palm of His hand. Yes, Virginia, there is a "higher power," but He or She isn't wearing a red suit and a fake white beard with a slightly sweet sickening whiff of alcohol on His breath. That caricature has been created for purposes of commercialism and has nothing to do with the YHWH of whom we are speaking when we refer to God. It is sad, and worse than sad, that large church organizations have fallen into this trap. They, like the Pharisees of old, have become wound up in stories and traditions of Western Civilization and wandered away from the path of the Spirit followed by the first-century Christians. And God is blasphemed among the unbelievers on this account. See Romans 2:24. If we celebrate the birth of Jesus at all, we should do so with sad reverence because God is making this sacrifice because of our weaknesses.

It is because of these fallacies that we are ashamed but powerless to save ourselves. As everyone in recovery knows, once a person is "hooked" he usually cannot escape without help. And the twelve-step program resorts to a "higher power," which for many is Christ. But many also are so turned off by "church" and "religion" because of all the confusion, denominations, rituals that are not founded in the Bible, the arguments among believers (see 2 Timothy 2:23), and hypocritical demands for cash that they find it nearly impossible to trust Him. The reason they cannot just trust Jesus is that church organizations and others have used and pushed manmade

[43] See 2 Samuel 11:1-4, for example.

doctrines of "religion," a poor substitute for Christ,[44] all our lives and these unbiblical ideas arouse suspicion and rebelliousness in people. We have in many cases pews full of good people, confused and lost, wondering "Why do bad things happen to good people?" and other such utter nonsense.

A knowledgeable Christian knows hard tests are not "bad things" any more than a naughty child is a bad person, an alcoholic street person no more of a sinner than the preacher's adulterous wife. The truth is no one can fix himself—not even one. See Ro. 3:10-20. Not by meditation, self-help courses, yoga classes, vegan diets, or any other power that we possess. Only Jesus Christ can fix us. See Romans 9:16; 30-33; and 10:3-10.

So why can't I preach a worldly utopia of saved people, transformed by the blood of the lamb? Several reasons jump out. I'm sure there are more.

I must be honest, starting with the fact that I am too leaky a vessel; I still must be purified like silver. That is to say, the ore is placed in a crucible and heated by fire and the metal comes out. The rest, the dross, is scraped off and cast out. And I will be thrashed like wheat, which is scattered on the thrashing floor and beaten until the edible seed is separated, the chaff is taken out with the winnowing fork, and burnt in the fire. And I must be tested because faith untested is no faith. I have been tested a little but much more testing is required to perfect my faith. I have yet to prove out, to pass God's assay, to be genuine in other words, not fools' gold. The Risen Christ, Judge of the world, is no fool. See John 5:21-30; John 9:39-41; Romans 5:6-10. So, I have hotter fires to walk through, and much individual suffering ahead. And if by His Grace I finish the race and pass the test, *only* then will I be anything; but of course, then I will have to leave you. Taking up the cross and following is like this. And no, I am not courageous enough to withstand it. Most of you readers have far more bravery than me. I must pray for courage when the going gets rough. I cannot stand on my own, but God can make me stand and I pray He does.

Second, everyone is at different rungs of the ladder as we are climbing. Some are more advanced than others. The slow exasperate those farther along; the ones who have gone farther have to guard against the devil so that

44 See 2 Timothy 3:4, a "form of Godliness," yet denying its power. I think this is what you get with a watered-down gospel. People going to church on Sunday, but not being led by spirit, instead thinking the worldly institution has them covered. And unbelievers wondering how anyone can believe what appears to be nonsensical, while neither group understands the Bible.

they don't discourage those struggling behind. For if we persist, we will all reach the same place. And no one can boast before God. Refer to Matthew 20: 1-16. The meaning of the parable of the workers in the vineyard is that those who come late, even those who are slower, will be counted the same as the super workers who started at the beginning, and accomplished great things. There is no room for pride. And this is "fair," because "we" accomplish nothing on our own, and every Godly accomplishment is really God working through us. God does not judge as the world judges; God sees the heart. But woe to those who are lukewarm. See Christ's word to the church in Laodicea in Revelation 3 (paraphrasing) "We are not taking in any halfhearted hypocrites. Sorry. You all have some work to do before you will be fit for the Kingdom. But keep working on it. It can still be done. With God everything is possible."

Most importantly, *God already has the perfect world all arranged for those who pass the test.* It is described in Revelation 22. We cannot usurp God's prerogative by trying to create it ourselves.

All the theories of utopia are worldly, and people's efforts to create them are worldly, because they all center on the issues of money and power and the laws of human beings. It doesn't work because we cannot be both worldly and spiritual. The priests and the Pharisees had Godly laws, but they were worldly men. See John 7:24; "stop judging by mere appearances and make a right judgment."[45] Jesus is asking the Pharisees to look beyond the superficial appearances of things and base their judgments on the heart and spirit and intent of the laws. This lack of a deeper insight distinguishes a truly Godly person from someone attempting to simply follow a "cookbook" approach. The law, even a law written by God on stone could not be administered justly by men. Reading Acts 15, Peter says this. And the law was weakened by the flesh, or sinful nature; that is, the constant wanting of the physical body and mind. See Romans 8:1-4. If a worldly system of laws, practices and observances set up by God could not perfect (sanctify, make holy) mortal man, certainly nothing devised by weak, fallible, worldly men could fix people and render them righteous. And all men, even the most spiritual must sometimes be worldly by necessity, in their needs to eat, to keep warm, and to reproduce. Man cannot outsmart

[45] Also see 2 Corinthians 3:14-15.

God or improve on His plans. Paul discusses this in Romans 9:16-29. God had it worked out all along. He designed it to play out. The answer lives in the spirit as God always knew and therefore the plan was always Jesus. We see it in Melchizedek in Genesis 14:17-20, and in Genesis 22, the ram whose horn was caught in the thicket. We see it in Hebrews 7, in Jesus the High Priest Forever, and in the Passover Lamb; and He is the substitute sacrifice for our sin in Romans 8:3-4. All the prophesies and the laws are fulfilled in His trial, execution, and resurrection. And He was here from the beginning. See John 1:1-5.

Therefore, no living human, priest or psychiatrist can fix us. Nor can any government, no matter how good the intention, repair or perfect the social order of men. Every worldly solution devised by human beings fails before it begins.

Yet, for the saved, there remains a loose sort of society consisting of those who are fully given over to Christ in their hearts and led by the Holy Spirit. They do not have fixed rules, but the guidelines we must live by are in the New Testament, and the law in the human heart. First and foremost, we must love God and love one another. This is the greatest commandment, and it is in the gospels, and it is reiterated by the writings of Paul. See Ro. 13:8-10. But this only works for Godly, spiritual people. We must be careful. Love is not lust. There must be no sexual immorality. The love we are permitted is described in 1 Corinthians 13:1- 13. We have always known the difference between right and wrong, even before Moses. See Romans 1:18-20. The Christian must fight temptation, resist the pull of the five senses, put on the full armor of God. See Ephesians 6:10-16.

Would you in any way harm someone you love in this selfless way? Would you steal from them, bear false witness against them, cheat them? You know right from wrong. And Christ admonished us in strong terms not to neglect the poor. See Matthew 25:31-46. See also Isaiah 1:11- 22, where God sets forth the errors of Israel.

But we—those who are saved and who have received the Holy Spirit—are not "under the law" as Paul puts it. See Gal. 5:1-6. We can eat any food, worship any day or every day; we no longer need to sacrifice animals. See Colossians 2:16-19. We are no longer required to count the phases of the moon or sacrifice sheep in a worldly tent. We should be wiser than to bow before any graven image, because it is just rock or wood and has no life in it. See Romans 1:22, 23; Nor do we bow to any creature for it only lives by God's grace, nor to any person for we are all equal in Christ. See 1 Corinthians 3:1-10. But whenever we serve, we should serve *only* Christ.

No worldly priest is anything more than the rest of us because we have Jesus Christ, the Great High Priest. See Heb. 4:14-16. He is the only one with power to clear our consciences and bring us into God's presence by the power of His blood. See Hebrews 9:12-15. The Levitical Priesthood ended 2,000 years ago, because with the destruction of the Second Temple, they had no place to be sanctified, or to perform the blood rituals, and because no one anymore is a clear descendant of Aaron. Other than Jesus and Melchizedek, there is no other priesthood established by God except the priesthood of every believer in Jesus Christ. The vestments God gave the Levitical priesthood are the only ones He ever gave, and everything had to be sanctified with blood in the tabernacle (tent) or in the temple. Further, only one place was authorized for the permanent temple, the spot where the Wailing Wall still exists, a bitter relic of the Hebrews of old.[46]

And certainly, the priesthood given to Moses by God with fire and thunder was incapable of *saving* anyone, and if so, then a priesthood that has been instituted by men 300 years after Christ is not capable.[47] If it were, then Christ died for nothing. If performance of some ritual or pronouncing some words in ancient Latin or Greek or sipping some wine could save, then why the scourge, why the thorns, why the nails? In fact, "works" (rituals, incantations, sacraments) cannot save anyone. See Romans 9:30-33. Neither the works of the law; rituals, feasts, sacrifices of the Hebrews, nor the works of churches: rituals, liturgies, chants, and repetitious prayers; nor any sacrament or incantation can save; nor can any gift of alms no matter how much is given.

[46] I spent several chapters in *Twice Blessed: First Century Christians in a Twenty-First Century World* explaining this issue and all the reasons modern Christians are not bound by the Law of Moses. The Bible goes into great detail on this in Acts 15, Hebrews, Galatians, Colossians, and other places.

[47] This does not mean that those who attend and believe in their churches are not saved; but it is their faith that saved them, not these worldly practices.

What *can* save? A sincere conviction that Jesus Christ is the Son[48] of the Creator of the universe, belief that God raised Him from the dead, and surrender of our lives to Him. And where does that leave us? What do we do now? This was my own question having no one to guide me after I met Christ in person; and, with no example to follow, the only place I could turn was to the Bible itself. Clinging to my belief, I read John, chapters one through six over again. Convinced that Christ had appeared to me in a vision, and it was not just a fantasy, I reasoned that next I would turn to Romans, not that I really knew much about it. The church had never really taught it in a unified, systematic manner. It was here that I first got a picture of what it was supposed to be about, and of the meaning of Christ's higher teachings. These were eye-opening. As I studied, I realized that we are spiritual beings, not of the flesh, and that the purpose of this existence in the house of flesh was to grow us and prepare us to be with our father and to be brothers and sisters to Christ, and joint heirs in the kingdom. Gal. 4:3-7.

In summation, I can testify that just as meeting Jesus Christ completely changed my life, really reading and studying the Bible changed all my ideas about church, about so-called doctrine, about the entire concept of religion as currently practiced in mainstream church organizations.

I realized that none of these organizations were actually started by the people who knew Jesus in the flesh. Some make that claim, but it is not in my Bible. Nor did first century Christians practice a set liturgy. They had a simple gospel as spoken by Paul in Acts 13. See also 1 Cor. 1:17-19. And they used Paul's letters as a form of instruction when they had them. Mostly, the churches relied on leadership from Paul, Silas, Timothy, and others who were taught by Paul, who received his gospel directly from Jesus Christ. Galatians 1:16-17.

Human beings want to establish order, formulate a simple, reproducible answer. We want to make it easy, but it was never supposed to be easy. And, just like our attempts to formulate a perfect government, or a perfect society, our attempts to set up a perfect church where all you

---

[48] This is in His human form, as we know Him, so that men can believe in Him. And He is both the suffering, kind, forgiving Christ and the resurrected powerful Christ with all the power of Heaven and Earth at His fingertips. He is both the crucified and the avenging, the humble and the glorious. Whether He is also anything else in relation to His Father-Creator, we do not know. But to all of us, He is our Savior and Redeemer, our High Priest Forever. We tend to see Him in our dreams and visions as the One who dies willingly for our salvation.

must do is follow a set formula, are doomed from the outset, because we are still just fallen, weak human beings. Jesus, the Risen Christ, is the High Priest Forever in His church. He is available to every individual for a one-on-one session everywhere and at any time. You must be sincere. You must be open. For most of us we will see most clearly when we are at the rock bottom of our lives, willing to do anything to get out of where we have gotten stuck. I'm not saying that is true for everyone, but I think for most it is in my experience. All of our pride must be crushed out of us like grapes in a wine press, whether we are saved first or not. And there is no faking it—He sees right through us. Nothing is hidden. Confession is more about coming clean with oneself than telling Him. He saw it all—everything you ever did and suffered right with you. And you needn't worry, because God will find the way to remove your pride in the trials of life if you are His.

The Bible, a collection of the writings of the ancient Godly people who had experience directly of God, demonstrates this over and over, from Cain and Abel through Revelation Chapter 3, Christ's message to the church in Laodicea. A friend once told me the Bible is a book of faith, written by men of faith for people of faith. I see it as a collection of writings by *spiritual* people, especially the New Testament, to help us seek spiritual truth. I think we are both right. And it is divinely inspired, and the writers and translators are helped by the Holy Spirit to get it right, and as it says in Ephesians we are engaged in spiritual warfare, and *anyone* who tries to shake your confidence in your Bible is being controlled by your enemy, and you must be separated from them, even people you love with a true heart if you cannot convince them.[49] The Holy Spirit will reveal the truth to you as you read your Bible. Believe that. The Bible you have is the one God intended you to have and you are to learn from it, not critique it. Find the one that speaks to you, learn to love it, and read it often.

I find that church organizations are worldly. They constantly demand money, and when they receive it, they do not use it for the poor in many cases, but for themselves, for fancier buildings, expensive choir robes and other trappings that were not part of the practice by the Christians of

[49] There are groups, especially on the internet pushing conspiracy theories calling into question the veracity of the Bible and the English translations. *Do not listen to this*. The internet is not a reliable source. Conspiracy theories, by definition, are incapable of really being tested and therefore proliferate. Anyone who tries to tell you that your Bible is not trustworthy is *dangerous* and deceived. Do not listen to them!

Paul's day. Some churches are so materialistic they remodel the building every ten years, and the demand for more money never stops even though they have million-dollar endowments. And they believe the million-dollar endowment and the upscale trappings, and the million-dollar German-made pipe organ are signs of Godliness, although, when viewed in spiritual clarity, they may be just the opposite. The Bible is the only completely reliable source, and your revelations in the Holy Spirit, as long as they are foursquare with the Bible, are the information you can count on. And that brings me to the subject of materialism.

Chapter Nine

MATERIALISM: THE RELIGION OF EVIL.[50]

This is not fun for me to write about, because I like to focus on the peace, blessings, and joy we have in the Holy Spirit. However, I think I have greater insight into this partly because my father was a convinced Marxist, and I grew up knowing the ideas of Marxism and knew about it from childhood. Also, since Marxists do not believe in God, because they are materialists, I grew up with the arguments of atheism, and had to defend any belief I had in argument with my father, who was a Phi Beta Kappa with triple majors in mathematics, chemistry, and physics.

In Eve's story we explored how she was seduced by "sin" or worldly desire and sin entered the world. And as we see from the stories of Cain and Abel, Sodom and Gomorrah, David and Bathsheba, the history that resulted from worldly desire. And the mature realize that sin is more than just breaking the rules. This is clear from the Sermon on the Mount in Matthew 5, wherein Jesus discusses the heart attitudes and internal

[50] Materialism is a philosophy which holds that the material world is all that exists. Matter, energy, and the physical laws account for everything, and there is no spirit or spiritual reality. Existentialism and physicalism are forms of materialism. Marxism and communism and other so-called "utopian" theories take this as a given and set about to perfect human society based on the idea that if there is no God or afterlife, the best humanity can do is effort to create a better physical world. Unfortunately, these always wind up being coercive and power-driven. The idea that the lofty goals justify the means by which they are accomplished leads to loss of freedom, harsh treatment of individuals and even mass murder.

psychology of sin in a way very different from the Ten Commandments, and the several hundred other rules and regulations in the code of Moses[51] contained in the Torah. Simply the fact that you have not murdered anybody or committed adultery will not get you into heaven. God judges the *heart*. Sin is the result when worldliness and desire, which are the root of these acting-out manifestations of sin, enter the mind and cause us to venerate the material world and is the reason we need rules and prohibitions in our society. But for the wickedness, rooted in desire and worldliness in our hearts, these would not be necessary. See Gal. 3:19; Ro. 13:8-10. Before a person murders his wife, or embezzles from his employer, the sin must grow in his heart for a long time.

It is helpful to understand that there are two kinds of "wrong" In law; *malum in se* means a thing is wrong in itself, even if there is no law; and *malum prohibitum* means a thing is wrong simply because the law or some authority declares it wrong. Murder is an example of *malum in se*.[52] So, the codification in the law to not murder is there for the people who have evil in their hearts so that they can receive their just punishment. The righteous do not need it, because they haven't got murder in their hearts.[53]

The prohibition to the Hebrews against eating shellfish is *malum prohibitum*, wrong because they were prohibited to do it. They were supposed to be undergoing purification[54] to become the bride of Christ. See the parable of the wedding feast in Matthew 22. But it was never *evil—malum in se*—to eat shellfish. People get very confused over this. But for those under the law two thousand years ago, there was no difference. The Torah was the Torah, set in stone, immutable, unchangeable. Trimming a man's beard, eating pork, or working on the Sabbath were transgressions against the Torah. These may not be "evil" deeds in the same sense, but those who live by the law must obey the entire law. See Gal. 3:10; 5:1-3. This confusion causes people to focus again on the outer, neglecting the

[51] The written code contained over six hundred rules and regulations. Contrary to what many modern Christians think, breaking any of them or failing to perform ***any*** of the religious duties imposed by the law was equivalent to breaking the whole law. See Galatians 5:3; 3:10. So, in that sense trimming one's beard or eating steamed clams was as bad as breaking one of the Ten Commandments. The Torah was designed by God to set the Hebrews apart and to prepare the place to which He was going to send His Son, Jesus Christ.

[52] In Genesis chapter four, Cain "sins" by murdering Abel, even though there were no written laws at that time.

[53] See Ro. 13:8-10.

[54] In ancient times, a betrothed virgin would be separated or sequestered, kept pure at her father's home, while she waited for the groom to finish their home and come to claim her.

inner, and blinds them to the spirit, just like the priests in John 9, the story of the man born blind. See John 9; Acts 15:10.

However, for example, people *always* knew murder was wrong, even before there were laws. See Gen. 4: 10-12. This is part of the "knowledge of good and evil;" although there is much more to it than this. It is our seduction by the material world, the focus of our limited attention on the flesh and the material things, and the endless desire to please the flesh by giving the worldly flesh everything it wants. And what it wants is everything there is. Reading Matthew 4:1-11, we see clearly that Christ was tempted precisely because He was immortal, powerful, he could have ruled over all the kingdoms of the earth forever, taking whatever He wanted, and all would have bowed before Him. And any who did not would have suffered terrible consequences because of the ultimate power he would have had if only He would surrender to worldly desire, which is a form the devil takes when he seduces people. And the intoxication of such power, through surrender to the devil, would have made Him a slave forever to evil. At least that is what the devil seems to be after in Mat. 4:8-9. However, in His humility and obedience He chose to obey His Father and humble Himself, and die a mortal death, that He might be raised as King of Glory and rule a kingdom of righteousness forever, in harmony with the Creator. And that was *always* God's plan, set in place from the foundations of the world.

Eve was seduced by the world, the physical, the tempter. The devil teaches people materialism, the false belief that the physical is all there is, that death is the end; that there is no spirit and no Creator. Its evil is double because the devil certainly knows this is all a lie, but he is a liar and the father of lies. John 8:44, 45. The ordinary idolator sins by placing (in his mind) something equal to or greater than God; but the materialist erases God entirely. The victim thinks everything has always just been here. The universe is a bunch of dumb rocks flying aimlessly around space crashing into one another. And life is senseless, pointless, meaningless. Is it any wonder that such people tend to be angry and bitter, eaten from the inside by the accumulated hurts of a life in the flesh, and thinking that they got a bad deal, that it is all terribly unfair?[55] That no "just God" could possibly do this to me.

Such people seeing life in materialist terms may conclude that all that matters is "me," the worldly self, the flesh. And we worship the self, our imaginary self we each see in the mind, smarter, braver, stronger, and more beautiful than we really are, and greater than all others (imitation of Lucifer; see Isaiah 14:13-14.). People believe in the idolatries of success, money, power, and fame. All fawn obsequiously over those who have worldly fame and ignore those who have not. If a person believes this, it is logical to be narcissistic and selfish. See James 2:1-7. We get one crack at this life, and he wants to get everything he can out of it, but for himself only, or maybe his family, but some are willing to "win" through betrayal or even murder, since they are not held accountable. Furthermore, when the truth is revealed—the sin of a famous or powerful person—people swarm like sharks at the feeding. The billionaire who ran a Ponzi scheme and robbed his friends of their life savings in their old age, leaving them impoverished; the movie star who went to prison; and especially the minister of God who was embroiled in a sex scandal. All meat for the tabloids.

Even those with better instincts, however, become misguided in their "good intentions." Even the well-intentioned socialist is willing to trample the rights of individuals in order to achieve his ideal of the "greater good" for the "masses." They are convinced of the logic of the greatest good for the greatest number. They do not understand that good intentions cannot justify evil means.

We live in these houses of flesh so that its wants are with us from birth. As quickly as we satisfy one wanting, it wants something else. It does not stop wanting until it dies and returns to the earth from which it was made. It is of the earth and belongs to the earth; it is fed from the earth, and it returns what it receives to the earth. It is something we possess briefly; given to us to fulfill God's plan and his word and to demonstrate his power. It is full of amazing powers of its own, the five senses, the power of locomotion, the power to make and use things in the material world to sustain itself; it also has the power to reproduce, to make more like itself; and above all it

[55] Often, these people think life has been unfair to them specifically, and that if there were a God that He singled them out individually to suffer. A Christian realizes that everyone has his own cross to bear, and that each suffers in his own way.

has power to understand and reason and make choices. All these powers are exclusively in the material realm, but there is one more that is greater than all of them. That is, the power to connect to the Creator and to be in a relationship with Him, but *only* if He consents. Therefore, the Bible frequently uses the analogy of a wedding to explain our relationship to God. See Matthew chapter 22:1-14. And this is because inside each of us God has put the eternal spirit. God's true nature is spirit; and so is ours. See John 4:24. The spirit wants to be united with the Spirit. See Ro. 8:22-25.

In this twenty-first century we, those who are at least trying to do what is right, are devoted to growing our children, educating them, protecting them, and taking them to practice sports or band, all to help them in a worldly sense. Often, however, we devote too little attention to the development of a strong connection to God, our creator. And the government schools and television and the media constantly preach the deceiver's message. I made all these mistakes and regret them, but I had hoped the church would teach them. This is no excuse or justification; I failed in this respect. I could not give them what I did not possess myself.

If you read the book of Ecclesiastes, you will see that every form of worldly pursuit is fruitless in the end; therefore, materialism is false and leads to nothing but death of the spirit. Paul explains in Romans, chapter eight that to set the mind on the things of the world is spiritual death. People since Eve have always been seduced by Satan, who uses our worldly desires to blind us to the spirit; and all the distractions of worldly existence to keep us enslaved to worldliness. The distractions we receive through the eye and the ear, the demands on our time, the pleasures of the flesh have multiplied exponentially through the twenty-first century. Often, we are too busy or just plain exhausted to seek God. And the fate of worldly man is sealed. This, the above descriptions of basic worldly thinking, are what I call the soft form of materialism, characterized by consumerism, and the desires for things, and the self-idolatry of "lifestyle," is a very sneaky trap for human beings. It is like quicksand. Once you fall in, it's hard to get out. It's like a maze because the search for an exit without a guide can leave a person frustrated and desperate and in the end every path pursued just leads to death, as both Ecclesiastes (Solomon) and Paul (in Ro. Ch. 8) warned us. This is the universal fate of the worldly man. When a man dies people go through his things, keep some, sell some, and the rest they trash or donate to the poor. And these are the things for which he struggles all his life—now as lifeless as his flesh. Scrooge was shown this by "the ghost of Christmas future" in Dickens' A Christmas Carol, as he saw people dividing up his belongings after his future death. If you have had a parent die, you know the drill.

Furthermore, do not imagine that philanthropy is a release from this prison. A man can create a monument to himself or put his name on the cornerstone of a building. In one hundred years, no one will care; friends and acquaintances will forget him quickly. Most of my friends in law practice for thirty years have moved on and even when I was looking for mediation business were not very interested in me because there were bigger names in the arena. Even family will pass, leaving only a couple of old photographs for the grandkids or great grandkids. All is vanity, rubbish, ashes—nothing.

No matter how famous you become, your worldly glory will fade over time.[56] Your beauty lasts a moment if that is your idolatry. People revel in sensuality, wallowing in the filth of the flesh. They gorge themselves with food, make themselves drunk on alcohol, brag about their money, vast amounts that are in reality the chains that bind them. And as they gradually realize that all this is temporary, they take pills and seek psychiatry to alleviate their anxiety. Their so-called "lifestyle" is nothing more than the worship of the devil. Their guilt feelings and anxiety cannot be expunged by giving alms. The shallowness of their thoughts is exposed, and they hide their pain behind masks. Anxiety, depression, substance abuse, a sense of being driven, rather than led, outright fear, dissatisfaction with life, even suicide—these are all symptoms of a worldly life. But, like a maze or like quicksand, they cannot get themselves extracted. Many put on a brave face and dream of some future in which they take the money and run and live happily ever after. Some dream of winning the lottery. But those who win the lottery do not escape. Often, they lose all the money, and they are crushed and destroyed by it. There are studies showing that winning millions of dollars does more harm than good for most people.

56 How many people today are excited by movie stars of the 50s and 60s? The post-millennial generation may have heard their names, but they have so much access to more current content most have little to no interest in the movies and stars the baby boomers watched.

God intended the world to be like this. Only the spirit and its union with the greater Spirit of God matters in any lasting sense. All else is dross, chaff, nothing. It is here to be the field in which to grow the wheat, nor is any of it the wheat itself. The soil is fertilized by that which is ignoble so that the noble crop may grow out of it. But the soil must be cleansed from the grain produced, the spirit, before it is fit for the Masters' table. In this way also, the filth of the material world must be cleansed from people before we are fit for the Kingdom of God. We must be prepared by separation like thrashing, and our chaff thrown into the fire, and we must be purified by the flame. Thrashing is a violent, painful process. The analogy is a perfect one for the Christian. Only then will we be fit for God. So, for example, in the past 18 months I have been tested by the difficulties of producing my testimony in a book and trying to sell it; also physically, by three surgeries, nine days in the hospital with septicemia, a shattered right ankle, separation from two of my closest friends, who also were among my most important Christian mentors. Satan was testing me like Job to see if I could be induced to renounce God, or like Jonah, to shirk my callings for Him. God allowed it because in His wisdom He knew I would not fall away in these light and transient sufferings, even though the sadness for my dearest friends is still present. I forgive them, but it still hurts. It was a hurt I never expected, and do not fully understand, but we bear up under these things like soldiers. See 2 Tim. 2:3.

However, there is a hard materialism which takes even more destructive forms. Founded on philosophies like existentialism, but without moral compass it also leads to implementation through communism, Nazism, fascism, and other harsh systems. This is the hard doctrine that states there is no God, life is suffering because the wrong people are in charge, and the state is what matters. They claim to pursue the greater good to the greatest number ("masses"). For this reason, they claim to be justified in just about anything they do for this "glorious" cause. The individual, individual liberty, property, and dignity can be trampled in order to achieve their goals.

Existentialist philosophy says that, since there is no God and life is suffering and death is final, the only real question is whether to commit suicide.[57] The communist doesn't want to commit suicide but thinks a better world can be created by fallible human beings. This requires the use of force, because as Frank Zappa once put it, "people like to own stuff." So, the result is that they believe the end justifies the means, up to and including theft and homicide. And since they are completely blind to God, there are no rules; or if there are rules, they can be justifiably set aside for the cause.

I should stop here and speak to those who think rules are necessary for saved Christians and are still confused about the law of Moses. As stated previously, in Romans 13 Paul explains that a saved person led by the Holy Spirit doesn't *need* rules to tell him not to murder, rape, kidnap, envy, slander, or steal. And in Matthew 5, Jesus explains we must purge all this worldly evil from our own hearts—a complete *transformation*—to enter His Kingdom. Not just by the obvious prohibitions in the law, even those which are *malum in se, but a transformation of the mind.*

To be led by the Spirit of God, however, means to trust that God would never lead anyone to engage in anything that is evil, if that individual were truly His and loved Him and loved his fellowman. Thus, we who belong to Christ owe no one anything beyond the duty of love (Ro. 13:8); although the unsaved and those whose faith is weak will still need rules to make them aware of sin, and the devil uses small sins and guilt and shame to ensnare them; and he also uses the unsaved to tempt and destroy Godly people. And, since we who are *relatively* more mature in faith also sin, though we never mean to do so, the rules of behavior are worthy of our study, important guidelines for self-reflection. So, if someone comes along with a clever argument for sexuality outside of marriage as a righteous path, we fall back on the Bible, and its authority to rebuke such a person. But Jesus doesn't care what you eat, and you can work in a Godly way on any day. (See Mark 7:1-23; Romans 14:1-12; 1 Corinthians 8:1-12; Colossians 2:6-22.)

On the other hand, the communist or other materialist acts out of love for neither God nor man, but for the advancement of a human-conceived utopia. He is one who thinks he has some brilliant idea, and that his idea is superior to God's idea. (Another form of imitation of Lucifer.)

---

[57] Famous question posed by existentialist philosopher Albert Camus.

He believes his own idea is so brilliant that he thinks whatever he does is justified no matter who it hurts. The principle of the greater good, or the perfection of human society is so important that the sacrifice of human rights of a relative few people, or even the deaths of millions, are fully justified, given the amount of senseless cruelty existing in this world. And, he has a point there, except that what he is trying to do is impossible, and his motives are worldly. Man was created by God; God has the formula for the perfection of man, and nothing in all creation can supplant God's plan. Furthermore, God's plan has been in place from the foundations of the world. See Ephesians, chapter 1.

The leaders of these materialist cults are worshipped as gods in some places. History and the Bible are rewritten by the state, as has been done in China now, and the devil's version is used as propaganda for the state. For example, in China, the story of Christ and the woman caught in adultery was rewritten such that Jesus stones the woman to maintain the social order. The real Jesus stood the established social order on its head.

The communist mind cannot fathom the parables of the lost sheep and the lost coin. They are so brainwashed that they see anyone having excess beyond his or her immediate need as immoral in itself. History is also rewritten. Some people want to re-write American history as a story of racism and exploitation. So instead of the pioneer spirit we see subjugation and genocide. Instead of courage and faith, kids are taught that our country is based on racism, and this leads to cancel culture and destruction of national monuments. It also directs people to think in terms of materialism and communism, to forget that God is sovereign over all things.

Fifty years ago, a communist named Saul Alinsky wrote a book called Rules for Radicals. He dedicated his book to Lucifer, which is entirely appropriate because Lucifer is the "prince of the air" and stands for all the false material values and principles of this worldly existence. He stands for all the motivations that cause men to do evil and for all the flashing lights and distractions that cause people to be confused and unable to see spiritually. He stands for everything that misleads and entraps people and causes them to get stuck, the idea that life is about "me;" that feeling good is more important than doing good; that my "success" is more important than other people; that "more is better." And of course, Lucifer stands for the idea that it Is people who will create a "better world," rather than God.

Alinsky, in Rules for Radicals, set forth how to undermine our principal institutions, infiltrate government, education, and the church. Reading it, I saw into the mind of an evil genius. Inspired by Satan, all his "rules" have been carried out in whole or in part at this point in the early twenty-first century. I must admit that I don't know very much really. But I am certain that communism is evil per se. Under communism the state is above all, and the central committee of the Communist Party makes the final decisions on absolutely everything. Control is essential. And the rights of individuals must be surrendered for the "greater good." That is to say, the government can take away everything, cast anyone into prison, starve entire provinces or countries, reduce the entire society to subsistence level poverty, and execute political dissenters all in the name of some nebulous undefined greater good. And socialism is just a longer, slower glide path into communism. That is, over several generations the government takes over more and more aspects of life and brainwashes children until all vestiges of individualism and liberty are gone and the central government controls everyone and rules without checks and balances. Politically incorrect speech is a crime; dissent is not tolerated, and Christ is never spoken of—although a monument to Lucifer in the town square is allowable.

All these things, and fascism, Nazism and other extreme forms necessarily require complete control and central planning to be carried out. And that means suppression of dissenters and oppression of religion. Nothing can be above or equal to the state, or to the "greater good."

For this reason, our politics is a cesspool, which is a fact Christians need to understand, lest they fall prey to its seductive wiles. I do not say we should stay out of politics, just that we must be very prepared and have on the full armor of God. See Ephesians 6:10-16.

In saying this, we also must understand that we are not the ones who win. God wins. Our tasks are led by the Holy Spirit, and we do spend time with God and ask God for guidance in all matters. He leads us, and we walk by faith, not by sight. We follow the light of Christ and walk in his footsteps even to the cross. So, we must be careful about the morass of twenty-first century politics. If we take a side, we must be aware that neither side is the be-all or end-all, and that all people are broken, fallen, and prone to sin. And they will destroy good men and women who are unprotected without even intending to do so. God is the Alpha and the Omega, the beginning, and the ending. And in the Bible, we see His one story, one plan, one way. For those of us who believe it in our hearts, it is the only way. See John 10:18. So, we must be aware that sometimes God's plan may call for our side to lose, even if we were in the right. God sees all ends, we do not. We pray for His will to be done, but do we really mean it, or are we secretly hoping for Him to do our own will?

God's judgment has already been rendered on this world, on its leaders and on the "prince of the air." Materialism was doomed when the devil taught it to Eve in the garden, so whatever you have—your house, your car, your money—will be lost to you one way or another, either in this life or in death. This is chaff, blown away by the breeze, or separated by thrashing and thrown into the fire. That is the painless part. But also, your physical body, your worldly relationships to other people, including your parents and children, everything in this world. In fact, Jesus said we will be set child against parent, brother against brother, as those who accept the gift will be persecuted, mocked, and reviled. We expect to be attacked by our friends for no reason, ridiculed for our belief, and fired for speaking out. The devil sometimes uses good people to do his dirty work, so look out. People may think they are Christian, but inwardly many are very materialistic. And whether someone thinks they are communist or capitalist, Christian or atheist, they can be tricked and manipulated by the devil who cares for no one and respects nothing.

Therefore, we cannot value anything in this world too highly, even ourselves. See Romans 12:3. We know that all goes on the altar and people lose things they really care about, people they really love, family and friends. And God is sovereign over all. It can be a bumpy ride. Life lasts as long as He says. The challenges of the world are what they are, both to the bad and to the good. For some they are harder than others. The issue of central importance is our response. When God gives us lemons, are we going to go around with sour faces or are we making lemonade?

Chapter Ten

A Better View

God is the Master!

People pray about their sufferings and about those of others, but they become confused if their prayer does not result in getting what they want. Many people miss the point. We are in a blind, unspiritual world. We are in temporary houses of flesh. We paid nothing for them, we didn't ask for them, we just received them as a gift, like the sunshine and the summer breeze. Like our mother's milk.

God is the all-powerful, all-knowing Creator of the universe and *everything* in it. He is sovereign over *all* things. The devil had to ask permission to test Job and Peter. God sees all ends; we do not. He created time and isn't confined by it like we are. Past and future are the same to God. We are here to fulfill His plan, which has been in place from the foundation of the world. Our personal plans are irrelevant. We want to be a doctor, a lawyer, or a businessman, live in a nice house with a nice family and drive nice cars. That might not be God's plan for our lives. Faith in Him means accepting when our plans are swept aside for His greater plan. We have the sure knowledge that there is a greater plan, and that the One who makes the greater plan knows what we do not know and can do what He says He will do.

So, we are permitted to pray for Him to cure our cancer, but we do so in deepest humility, knowing that isn't necessarily always His plan. Remember, we came into this world naked and bloody and screaming and helpless. Nowadays we have medicine to ease our passing, but even so, many leave in the same way. As even Christ did on the cross. Peter was crucified, and Paul was beheaded. If this isn't our example, what is? Jesus threw Himself on the ground. He asked the Father to give Him an alternative. (Matthew 26:36-39). But He accepted that there was no alternative in God's plan. I am certain He felt many of the same feelings I felt finding out my cancer can't be cured. He didn't want to die that way anymore than we would. He accepted God's plan.

But He did it for the love of us, and He did it in obedience to His Father's will. This fact is demonstrated in Genesis 22:1-18, and stated clearly in Ephesians 1, Acts 17:24-28, John 1:1-4, and many other places. God's plan required Jesus—gentle, loving Jesus—to die in this horrible way.

And we should be aware, our suffering and death may also be a benefit to us individually, that is, the real us, which is spirit, not flesh. See 2 Cor. 4:16-18. The body is just a tent, a temporary dwelling. To have faith is to understand that fact. Suffering perfects and refines us for the Kingdom of God, and death is the passage by which we exit this realm with all its evil and corruption and enter that better world. Spread your wings, angel. Shed the cocoon and show your colors. Rise in glory. But the flesh will always be afraid, because for flesh death is its end.

Now on this side of the river, divine healing does take place, but it is never just to benefit the flesh; it is usually to show the power of God, as in the healings performed by Christ in the Bible. If it is God's will to use me in this way, that is what will happen. But, if not, that is His will and plan for me. We walk in sorrow in this life, especially those most devoted to Him. Sometimes those deluded by Satan seem to have it much better, much easier, but in the end, they have already lost, and they will suffer the judgment. So, pray for them but do not envy them. And be happy for me, even if God never cures my cancer, because it was through cancer that I was brought to Him.

I would dearly love to have a few more years to be with you all, but I accept His decision if I do not, and I pray that everyone sees this as a perfectly acceptable outcome, not as a punishment; and certainly not as unfair. God is good, He is just, He is fair and most of all He loves us. We have rested in His gentle hands from the beginning, and he will not drop us, but will bring us gently and lovingly to Himself in the end.

Chapter Eleven

Street People

There is a very attractive part of being among the homeless; the ones who have been out awhile and have become streetwise. In saying this, I don't want us to overlook the hunger, deprivation, lack of access to medical care, basic hygiene, the belittling and making people "less than," physical violence against the homeless, and all the other things they suffer. Most of those who have developed the ability to live out here for a long time have learned to be relatively content with what they have, even though many people would look at them and say they have nothing. Don't get me wrong; most homeless people will explain that they really hate being homeless. And local governments carry on campaigns of cruelty trying to get rid of them. But people know that they can live better by accepting the situation and making the most of it.

Some carry all their belongings around in overstuffed bags, some stash their bedrolls and tents in campsites, and some just travel light having little more than a change of clothing, toothbrush, and a bedroll. It is especially tough on women. This world can be dark and cold and cruel. I have seen a couple of women who can physically defend themselves, but most are at the mercy of cruel people who are heartless and driven by rage or compulsion. And they can get hurt. If they are addicts or alcoholics, some are performing sexual acts in alleyways to pay for drugs. It makes me cry to think of what they are forced to do. But addiction does not take any excuses, it must be fed no matter what.

Added to all the other problems, there is currently a national trend of crackdowns and sweeps and ordinances that target the homeless. But, like I said, there are all kinds of people out here in the street. A lot of homeless people have jobs and families. Very few choose to be homeless. Divorce or breakup frequently leaves a man needing to find a place to live. Over 50 percent of Americans live paycheck to paycheck. Rents in our town have doubled in the last five years. Also, while wages have risen, they have not kept pace. So, an apartment in this town that was $700 a month is now up to $1200. Food prices are up 10 percent in one year, gasoline has doubled and used cars are at a premium. A person making as much as $20 an hour cannot always pay a security deposit, first month's rent and utilities up front, which is often the minimum required to rent an apartment. It can require as much as $3,000 up front just to get in and you still have to have something left over to live on. And especially with men, they often still have children to support. Once it goes to court, child support is deducted automatically from a person's paycheck, which makes it impossible for some to save anything. Usually, by the time a person is on the street, their credit is destroyed, and he can't borrow or save the means to become housed. The shelters are full of such men. And then there are the elderly and the disabled. They get a government check, but it cannot pay for what it costs to live, even minimally.[58] People eligible for government housing or rent assistance are on one year or two-year waiting lists. Some of these are seventy-year-old Vietnam-era veterans. A person may have a V.A. voucher for housing but be unable to locate a place that will take it, or they may be excluded because their background check isn't perfect.

Yet some of these people are relatively happy. One of the happiest people I met in shelter was a fifty-year-old divorced man who had been on the street for six years. People congregate on the street in places where they hope the police will not bother them, or in parks, under overpasses or bridges; and some panhandle, but most just don't want to be alone, because they are not safe. It is here that we do a lot of our work, reminding them of the presence of Jesus Christ, and that someone still cares. Many have remarked that our continued presence brings them hope. And the social organizations have resources to help people move beyond this if they are

[58] Some are as low as $900 per month.

willing and able. Many are not able to because of age, disability, or other problems.

At the same time, many people who live in big houses and drive fancy cars are miserable because they know, or in their hearts they suspect, that they spent forty or more years acquiring all that and now they're very soon going to lose it. They hope for a few years of retirement to enjoy it (like I did), but many drink alcohol or take pills for their anxiety, or for depression. It just doesn't seem fair. We work our whole lives away. We come to the office on Saturdays. I've worked Christmas Day, plowing through paperwork on cases I don't even remember. Is it any wonder so many lawyers commit suicide?[59]

Often, friends are fickle, families are dysfunctional, and only relatively few people are truly happy. Some may be in relatively happy relationships, but many are whistling past the graveyard. You might have a million-dollar house, but if you are drinking and taking pills to feel good about yourself, you are not a rich person. A rich person is one who is passionately on fire for God and for other people. One with love in his heart. And although writing a check may feel good for a moment, it doesn't last. It's better to be homeless than to live a lie. These things are all the result of materialism, the doctrine that denies all spiritual truth. For whatever reason—and everyone has lots of reasons—people sacrifice the spiritual for the material. That is one reason God required the blood sacrifices in the Tabernacle of Moses. God does not have any love for blood or burning animal fat on the altar. Read the first chapter in the book of Isaiah if you want to fact check that. He required these to force people to relinquish the material for the spiritual. And it was very imperfect, but it was the best the worldly man could do until the place and time was right for God to send His Son into the world to set things right and undo the damage Lucifer did in causing Eve to lose sight of the spirit and become lost in the life of the material world (flesh) forever. We must bear in mind that this was always Jehovah's way. This is the great drama He set up, acted out perfectly according to His plan.

And therefore God, who created everything, sent His Son so that the lost would be found. In Luke 15 the author recounts Jesus telling the

59 The practice of law consistently ranks among the top five occupations in rates of serious depression, anxiety, alcoholism, addiction, and suicide.

parables of the lost coin, the lost sheep, and the lost son.[60] The reason is this: the trick the devil played on Eve in Genesis has been played on *everyone*, and in many ways, using the material existence to blind us to the spirit, to our own spiritual essence and nature, and to the power of Yahweh the Most High God. The son saw the material wealth and chose it over the life that was given freely to him. When he found out through bitter experience that it was the wrong choice, however, his father accepted him with open arms. This is what God wants for each of us as well, and He is waiting. But He gave us free will. We must choose to forego our worldly pride and humble ourselves and He will throw an eternal feast in celebration for the return of the ones who were dead, but live again.

We are held prisoner by shame, guilt, regret, and anxiety. Images of future events the devil puts in our minds of negative outcomes that almost never occur at least in the form we imagine them; and guilt and regret over our past mistakes and choices, made while in a state of spiritual blindness. And all giving rise to shame, the belief that we are less than what we are. And we remain in this captivity, but Jesus, the Risen King comes riding in on His white horse with all the power and glory in Heaven and earth and saves us. See Revelations 6:1-2.

We are blinded in spirit and therefore led by the material wants of the flesh; and we live reactively responding to the events of the material world throughout our lives until Jesus, the Son of God and of man comes and restores our sight. See 2 Cor. 3:16. He alone breaks the chains that bind us and defeats the devil. See Isaiah 61:1-11. He intercedes for us with God as our Great High Priest. See Hebrews 4:14. He alone takes away our stinking garments and clothes us in white, bright, and clean, that we may stand before the throne of the Most High. While we are living in the tabernacle of flesh, He intercedes so that we can come into God's presence without fear, for He has poured out his own blood for us and He sits on the mercy seat to judge.

---

[60] I cannot overemphasize this point. God loves us all and He wants us all to be rescued, but He only accepts us if we submit to Him. See Ex. 19:5. He set up this world to be His field and we are His harvest. The good grain will be taken with Him but those who reject Him will be burnt in the fire, if they will not repent. He went to the extreme of sacrificing His own Son to save us. He set up everything to give us a second chance. You reading this are alive and able still to repent and turn your life over to Jesus Christ and be saved. ***You just have to be willing.***

There is a warning however: those who do not know and have not heard, but who are not evil at heart may be excused for things they do in ignorance. But those who hear and reject the salvation of Christ have no one to blame but themselves. We who are still living have time to repent. But this life often ends without warning. Therefore, *today* if you hear his voice, do not harden your heart. See Hebrews 4:6-11. You must turn away from the false doctrine of materialism and see that light has come into darkness; there is no choice for the enlightened. It is written that all the world will be made his footstool, and every knee will bend before him. The earth will cough up its dead from the ground or from the water or from the ashes or from the rocks and we will all stand before him to be judged. And every mouth will be sealed while he judges. He holds the keys to the Kingdom in His right hand and the winnowing fork in His left. No one may speak after Him. And His judgment is just. See John 5:30. See Revelations 19:11-17.

This is where we are, living in this physical world, suffering its never-ending cruelty—and we have heard the word of salvation. Through our Great High Priest, we have our door, and our one chance to change. See John 10:18. The past is forgiven, and the future is made free of condemnation for those who truly surrender to Christ in our hearts. See John 5:24.

For many, our biggest obstacle is doubt. The devil constantly sows seeds of doubt. Christians undergo months and seasons of testing, because of the devil's evil works. It has been my experience that it is best to confront these head on. As James cautions, proceeding without faith causes one to be double minded. And the assembly of Christians is also helpful to support faith, dispel doubt, and thwart the devil.

The most effective treatment for me has been to engage in my work with the people of the street. They not only sustain and renew my vision; they also provide me with opportunities to test my faith. One example was the pandemic. With God's help, trusting God's mercy, we got through this experience, and it helped me grow and test my faith through that winter of 2020 so that I felt sure in it. And I was not afraid, but rather exuberant every day, eager to do God's work. And during the time when everyone was concerned because people were getting deathly ill, there was no outbreak among our homeless in the shelter. Even though it was nearly impossible to enforce social distancing, and before there were any proven vaccines or treatments, God stretched out His hand over the homeless people. Very few among the ones in the shelter got Covid, and there was no case of spread inside the shelter or among its people. My heart is just overjoyed thinking about this, as the power of God is manifest to all who care to see it.

I must add that, while there is no such thing as salvation through works, clearly, salvation and faith are secured and perfected through work, testing, and challenge. As faith grows stronger the heart beats more truly; the body follows the spirit rather than the spirit following the body. The greater the challenge, the more the reward.[61]

The only limit is this: our good works must be based on love and compassion in the heart. See 1 Cor. 13:3. We are not benefactors to those we serve, but servants of God. Paul warns us against getting a high opinion of ourselves in Romans 12:3. So, if you boast, boast in God. Give credit, if there is credit, to the Holy Spirit. If you try to do these things without the Holy Spirit, you are likely to fail. But as you work in the Spirit, you will feel the power of the Spirit in you—at least that's how it went for me. Others may have different experiences, different feelings.

The street people provide me with an opportunity to test the things I believe, a possibility for the correction of the errors in my thinking, and the opportunity to "walk the walk." If I stray from the path, I find out because it is palpable on the street. They keep me honest, and I hope they help me to be humble. Many of them have grown in their own faith over the last five years and it is a blessing to see.

---

[61] Sometimes, I use an analogy comparing faith to a living plant. A plant needs three things: light, water, and food. The light we need is Jesus Christ. See John 9:5. The water is the Holy Spirit. See John 7: 37-38. The food is to do the work God has provided for us to do. See John 4:34.

Chapter Twelve

LIFE AND SPIRIT

I spent thirty years in the law working in stacks of papers during nights, weekends, and holidays. Overworked, overtired, relationships neglected, depressed, anxious, and unhappy. Then I retired. I went around the office with a lump in my throat saying goodbyes. I put my diplomas and awards into a box and took them home and put them in a closet. Ten years later, they are still in the same box in the same closet. They will remain there until I pass, and my survivors will sort through them. They may keep bits in their own closets, throwing away the rest. This is the fate of secular man. You hope your kids may visit more, but they have their own lives. You may have grandchildren, and they are a delight, but not everyone in America gets to see their grandchildren very often, and even if you do, they grow up. At some point they might put you in a nursing home when you get to be too much bother. I think it was these things as much as my cancer that made me see the reality of human existence with clarity. At some point these things we see happening to other people become all too real. Most of us never imagine ourselves in that situation. Further, to accept death, we need meaning. Not just a meaning for death, but a meaning for having lived at all. Surely, we will die whether we accept it or not, or whether it means anything or not. Acceptance in the light of understanding gives us the power to walk our walk in a way many people can't. To see meaning and purpose in everything makes it all worthwhile and brings an inner joy and peace to our existence.

I went to the emergency shelter with a bit of apprehension to be thrown in with the other people, the intoxicated, the ex-cons, the prostitutes, the ones society rejected, often from birth. Ninety-five people crammed into five thousand square feet to eat in one room and sleep in bunks crammed into every available space, plus twenty mats on the floor after the dining area was cleared. But I loved it and soon I loved them. The shelter was where I learned to let go and just let the Holy Spirit do the work, lead me, and give me words to say. And God took away my heart of stone and gave me a heart of flesh. And everything I gave I received back tenfold and hundred-fold. By the end of one year, I had healed people, held people, cried with people, and given my heart to people. I prayed with people. And the Holy Spirit of God did everything, it never was any effort at all. I was happy arising in the morning and excited going to bed at night, cancer notwithstanding. And that is how it was when I wrote my first book.

So, the serpent's trick played upon our mother, Eve, and handed down to the generations, gradually was being dispelled by the Spirit that Christ sent into the world of people for that purpose.[62] And this is also one of the reasons the meanings of the Bible, so obscure to me before were made clear to me and I was shown how it felt to let go and let God. Blessed day! I was no longer just my completely broken self; I was "me" as God intended. I was no longer rooted in the past, anxious about the future, too fat, too lazy, too selfish, and opinionated. I was a new creation in Christ, and I was deep in scripture all the time because I realized that scripture supported and helped in this personal transformation.

Abram, who became Abraham, was a descendant of Adam, living in the land of Ur, West of the Euphrates valley. He lived in this reality and the other simultaneously, although the flesh brain can only really focus on one at a time, and is always aware of this world, because it is made of the stuff of the world. Therefore, we can only see the spiritual world dimly most of the time. We do occasionally briefly visit the spiritual realm in visions and dreams and meditation, although at any time it is never far. See Acts 17: 24-28.

A person completely entangled in material life can be completely blind to the spiritual, which is the greater danger. This was Scrooge before he met

[62] If any atheist happens to read this, you can argue all you want about the issues of cosmology, evolution, and lack of proof. But these effects in my life experience are real and the fact that they have brought me joy and peace in this stage of life is inarguable.

the ghost of Marley in Dickens' A Christmas Carol. Even one penny, even one hour of work lost to the pursuit of more lucre on Christmas day was just too precious to bear. People can become like that—rich in worldly terms, but afraid even to enjoy their wealth for fear of losing it. Conversely, they can become slaves to physical pleasure, spending and borrowing what they do not have to keep giving the flesh whatever it craves. I have seen doctors, lawyers, and well-respected businessmen fall this way to drugs and sex. And others wind up bankrupt, committing suicide, or going to prison because they can't stand the pain of losing their status, wealth, or the admiration of the worldly community of heartless, fickle, worldly people. All these pursuits carried to these extremes are equally wrong and reflect spiritual blindness.

Some pious people can get so lost in their worldly pursuit of outward piety that they lose the ability to see what it was all about in the first place. They become sour and rule bound. A spiritual life is not a cake; It is not attained by following rules and rituals like a cookbook. This was the reason the "works of the law" that Paul admonished among the Hebrews cannot save anyone. Paul explains this in detail in Romans 9. But to those in modern Christian churches, the same principle applies. God is spirit and must be worshipped in spirit and in truth. See John 4:24. And people become proud in their piety; they start thinking they are special. I think this may be one reason some well-known people in popular ministries have fallen into sin.

The Bible teaches a different way of life, *humbly* led by the spirit. This is a life with very few rules or regulations, although it has admonitions and guidelines given, not to create more guilt for those whose sins are forgiven, but to guide and assist us lest we fall into sin and worldliness. We live by faith, guided by faith; whereas those who live by the law die by the law.[63] Those who live by the spirit have eternal life. See John 5:24, 6: 40. I lived with the burden of the worldly law and its regulations for many years, a lifetime. But, receiving the blessings of salvation, forgiveness, and the Holy Spirit relieved me of these chains and anchors.

The bottom line of this is that a weak inwardly neurotic and fearful person without Jesus can become a strong, brave, and sane person by the

[63] Gal. 3:10-14.

power of the blood, comfortable in this life here and now, as well as assured of life everlasting. If that is not good news, I don't know what is.

Now that does not mean God will give you everything you want. For desire is in all flesh. If you read Matthew chapter 5, this is what Jesus is talking about. If you are dreaming of winning Powerball and that is your idea of heaven on earth, forget it. In fact, you should not be gambling at all because it is an addiction and focuses all your attention on the bells and whistles and away from the Spirit of God. If you are dreaming about a fancy house, a sports car, and a supermodel girlfriend, you are entirely too worldly for the Kingdom of God. Beware, all these things lead to no good. You need to purge these images and get focused on better things.

It is exceedingly difficult for a rich man to enter the Kingdom of heaven. So, I would like it if God were to take away my cancer and let me live here another decade or so. But it is His choice. He is wise, I am a fool at heart. He is a loving father, and he knows what is good for me. Just like my boys when they were little, they never wanted to go down for a nap; I want to play in this world a bit longer. I prayed but he has not granted that one yet. I will find out when He pleases. I do feel He has kept me around because I am obedient, and He is using me. I accept his decision and his sovereignty.

God is God and Christ Jesus is His Son and the Holy Spirit is His gift. The living waters (spirit) flow from within the person who truly believes in Him. And they can be a beautiful thing, feeding and restoring His people and bringing those who wish to partake to the shores of the River of Life.

Our amazing God has put us here and leads us, you the reader, and me the writer to be here where we are at this moment. Everything that happened up to now has put us in perfect position for me to ask you whether you have met the Son of God as did the blind man in John 9:35-38, and received the gift of the Holy Spirit? He is near if you have not. Just as He was for me. And he is your Great High Priest to intercede for you with His Father. You need nothing else. No worldly priest or person, no ritual or incantation. It is not necessary to perform any magic trick or anything else. Just believe in him, surrender to him truly in your heart. But then, from now on you should confess Him and let others know you believe. Tell your story without shame. And be open to the spirit. Daily pray to be led by the Holy Spirit and listen for that "still small voice." If you get scared ask for the Spirit to give you courage. If you feel weak, ask Him to give you strength; If you feel disheartened, ask Him to fill your heart with hope.

As Paul says, adversity creates perseverance; perseverance, character; and character, hope. See Romans 5:3-4. So, expect reversals and pain as part of the process of growing the spirit inside you and purifying and testing you. Remember, when you suffer, Jesus sees you and calls you brother because he too has suffered. See Hebrews 2:9-11.

I have had challenges to face, but I am happy because they did not defeat me, and my faith in Jesus is how I got through even though the devil tried to tempt me. It does remind me of Paul's admonition throughout the New Testament, we must finish the race. We have no need to win. God wins. But we need to *persevere* to the end. We must remain strong both inwardly and outwardly in faith. The body can just go ahead and waste away, but the spirit is renewed day by day. See 2 Corinthians 4: 16-18.

Someone asked me the other day why Jesus had to die. And maybe implicit in that question is why do *I* have to die? And implicit in that is an honest confession that somewhere inside we all still harbor the same fear. Fear to let go, fear of the unknown. This is also the reason the Hebrews had to sacrifice their very best animals in the Tabernacle of Moses. First born male, one year old, without blemish. Nothing else would do. See Leviticus chapter 1; Malachi 1:6-12. And it is because of the seduction of Eve in Genesis 3:1-7. The spiritual Eve exchanged the Spirit of God for the physical world created by God. God is here waiting for us to disentangle from the world He gave us and exchange it for the Spirit that he has offered us from the beginning, but we are not doing it. We just can't seem to let go of it. It is so addictive; it feels so good.

Think about it. Many Americans live in nice houses, in nice neighborhoods, drive nice cars, wear nice clothes. That is, those of us that are middle class Americans. There are people who cannot afford such things all around us, living on our streets. Many middle-class people want to get rid of "those people" because they remind them of their shame. How much do our things mean to us? Would you be willing to give all your possessions to help someone else? A total stranger? No one expects that but as Dickens states in A Christmas Carol, the poor and the hungry are your business; they are my business. Turning a blind eye is forging a new link in your chain.

In saying this I'm not trying to add to anyone's personal guilt trip. In fact, guilt is absolutely the wrong reason for doing anything. The Bible is not about guilt. Jesus died to take away guilt, how can you go on feeling guilty? What I am asking is whether you could just be as happy or happier without your fancy house, your expensive car, and pricey vacations. Could you reduce your lifestyle to quite a simple life, drive an old jalopy, live in a little house in the hood, and be happy? Could you wear secondhand clothes and be happy?

We naturally tend to sell the spirit too cheaply, exchanging it for nicer and nicer worldly things. All of us, me included. Because the devil is a clever salesman. He shows up telling you that you need a better house, more expensive car, second house, trip to Italy or whatever he is selling. Just take your eye off the spirit and look down and you will need more of something. So therefore, Christ had to die to teach each of us to exchange the dross of this world for the spirit; To let go of the things we have which are just the dust of the earth, for what is better, permanent, and glorious with a light that does not fade over time.

You see, if you look at Matthew chapter 4, the temptations of Christ, he could have had it all. All the power, all the money, houses, women, and much more. But he chose the cross. His hands and feet spiked to pieces of lumber, hung up in shame, naked and mocked, bleeding, in pain. And there he died with no one to save him. But then God raised him from the dead; and He will raise us. He will not ask if we were rich or poor, black, or white, winners or losers. He will see inside of us, our hearts. For His gaze is "sharper than any double-edged sword, piercing to separate soul and spirit, joints, and marrow." Hebrews 4:12.

Letting go means seeing the truth, seeing things for what they are. And Christ sits in the judgment seat. And he does not judge like the world judges, asking how successful or how many or how much; He judges by a heart gauge asking how sincerely, how humbly, and how lovingly?

We will all stand there to be judged. This life is over in the blink of an eye and gone, and no amount of money donated, no amount of volunteer work can get past the judgment of the heart that says, "I gave everything for you—will you give everything for me?"

Chapter Thirteen

SUFFERING

I must tell you most of the valuable things I know were obtained through suffering which includes physical, mental, and emotional pain. One of my friends, a former US Marine, wore a t-shirt that said, "pain is the sensation of weakness leaving your body." The body is made of living tissues, blood, and muscle. As stress is judiciously applied, these get stronger and tougher. These improve the body when done as part of an orderly routine, and muscles will experience a sensation as they use up the last bit of oxygen and they will be sore the next day with built up lactic acid until the blood supply is able to clear it all and then you must step up your workout. This should begin as children and continue through life. It will enhance the quality of life and the gift God gave us in this body will be able to carry out its work if we keep it lean, toned, and strong.

In similar fashion, in many ways, the spirit must be worked and exercised to grow. But, unlike gym workouts, real life tends to be the proving ground of the spirit. It is a war. For people raised without a strong spiritual core and belief, and a daily practice, the shock of this war can overcome them and can be damaging. We are tested by severe things like divorce, loss of relationships, suicides of friends and family, loss of our jobs or businesses, bankruptcy, homelessness, and other serious life traumas which cannot be just passed off or ignored; and there are no "do-overs. Everyone says they are sorry. So as one friend expressed it to me, "What do I do with sorry?" Sympathy is natural, but sympathy is not much help. Only faith in God and in Jesus Christ can carry people through the real storms and tests of life, in my experience. Furthermore, we can become "shell shocked" over repeated emotional injuries. Some people will withdraw and become isolated as a result while others will turn to drink or drugs to kill the emotional pain.

Our faith should provide us with the spiritual equipment to handle these things and our church families should support us and comfort us in times of need.

Many churches fail to provide an adequate systematic preparation for *growth* through the unavoidable suffering we all experience in life. They don't like to talk about it because it is too "negative," and the object is to fill the pews and the collection plate. So, even when we are reaching out in mission, there is little reaching in—to those who are suffering with emotional, financial, and other crises *in* the congregation. We do have deacons and others who ask if everyone is "OK," but what is needed are friends—people we know and trust in a deeper way. Jesus said, "My command is this: that you love one another as I have loved you." See John 15:12. Now some may have small circles of friends within the church; but others may be isolated and suffering in silence, or ashamed to ask for help. I have a most unfortunate memory of one man in my church, a lawyer, who killed himself. I always feel guilty when someone I previously knew does this; why didn't I see? Why didn't I say something? We don't get "too personal," we don't "pry;" it is bad manners, bad form, we keep private matters private. We are afraid to embarrass one another.

Understanding suffering is one of the most important ingredients to a Christian life. Suffering fulfills many important functions in spiritual life. First, it is usually what brings people tearfully to the Risen Christ, ready to make a change. It grows and strengthens us in spirit. It tests us so that we know our faith is real. It purifies us from pride and other sinful attitudes. It teaches us to reach out to the Lord when times are tough.

But in many churches, we don't question, we rarely talk about the hard stuff. We are nowhere near discipleship if we don't apply it within the group. We need to become able to share in the group, and testimony of those who have had severe experiences and been rescued by our relationship with Christ paves the way. I was a sinner. I was afraid of dying and being condemned to hell. I feared the devil. Jesus Christ appeared to me in a vision and saved me from my burden that was killing me; that was far more deadly than cancer. Now, I can talk about that in front of a group. But not five years ago. Then, I was completely afraid.

Now, I understand that cancer, loss of loved ones, even divorce, and financial ruin are often much to our benefit in spirit; and that death is not the end. I now see that there is a purpose to all that goes on in this ever so cruel world.

Cruelty and hardship drive unbelievers to Christ; they deepen the faith of believers; they establish our relationship to the Father and our brotherhood with the Son and confirm our inheritance in the Kingdom.

But, as Jesus said, "God is spirit and must be worshipped in spirit and in truth." John 4:24. So the "form of godliness" referred to in 2 Tim. 3:1-5; 4:3-5 is found in the "nice church," often major denominations, where many are either like the Pharisees, following the outward but lacking in the inward *transformative* presence of Jesus, the Holy Spirit, and the full understanding of who God is, or else people are too polite or too ashamed to share the rough stuff. It is watery coffee, where you come and polish "your spot" in the pew every Sunday, attend church functions, sing in the Choir, help with group projects, put in your tithe, sing the songs, say the words, but not much else is required. And you may be made elder or deacon, and everyone greets you with an exaggerated smile and shakes your hand with a firm grip. "Nice to see you. Nice tie. Lovely day." This is also the time for "sorry;" "Sorry for your loss;" Nice.

But God is a vast, eternal, all powerful spirit, who called forth the universe including time, space, and matter, and set in place the physical laws.[64] He is the One who created us in his image and likeness, in other words as spiritual beings housed in a temporary house of flesh; and arranges everything to bring us to a point where we can reach out and find him though he is never far. He is never sorry; never weak, never fails. He does not come with sympathy and forced smiles. *We have physical things so that*

[64] I spent some time watching and meditating on images of Andromeda, with its estimated one trillion stars, and others of the galaxies in the known universe viewed through Hubble. God, our God, the Real God, did that. His power is awesome and mysterious and yet, He cares about ***you***. As far as we know, we are the only beings in this vast creation capable of knowing and appreciating who He is. Thinking on this I feel weak in the knees and humble before Him.

we can learn to lose them. We as descendants of the original couple have our eyes on the material and therefore, we must be taught that they are nothing next to the One who created everything. We create nothing; we are allowed to use His creation, but not to take pride in it.

But more than this, we see that we cannot do anything good ourselves, but He can do great things by using us as a carpenter uses a hammer and saw. We do not say "The hammer and saw built me a house or a boat." They are useful but easily replaceable. Expendable. They are nothing without the hand that wields them.

This is the reason there is no salvation by works. We cannot save ourselves by being nice. We must each be open and available as God has made us to do his work. Beyond this openness to his will, we can do very little. Like Abraham was when God called, and he responded "Here I am." See Gen. 22:1.

But God shapes and forges His tools. He sharpens His weapons. Like Corrie Ten Boom, whom He selected to inspire twentieth-century Christians. And he prepared her by forging her spirit under the hammer of the Nazis. He made her tough in the Holy Spirit; He gave her faith that could not be broken by anything—even death.

So too Paul suffered many beatings and tortures, as did many others, and so did the Wurmbrands, and so did Martin Luther King. And today, thousands around the world suffer this way. Yet they cannot be separated from the love of God in Jesus Christ. Romans 8:31-39 states that we are more than conquerors. We are not all called upon for this kind of sacrifice, but we are bound to our Lord no matter what happens.

Chapter Fourteen

NOT AGAIN... THE TOMB IN THE PORTABLE TOILET

I wasn't going to publish this story, but it is part of the overall experience that I am sharing, and it is a story that needs to be told so that a poor kid will not have died in vain.

My heart hurts this morning. Another kid dead—I think of the young ones as kids because they are the same age as my sons. Thirty-two years old, living on the street, nice young guy, smart, talented.

And what was his tomb? A portable toilet next to a construction site downtown. Christ lay two days in a stone tomb wrapped in linen with fragrant herbs. This boy, one year younger than Christ lay two days in a locked portable toilet.

Christ was pierced in his hands and feet. This young one was pierced everywhere, by the tracks of needles bearing poison. Surely Christ will plead his case to the Father.

Which of the four horsemen brings this curse upon us? Is it the Black Rider, with his scales, grinding the faces of the poor? Or perhaps the Conqueror on the White Horse driving it on to pay for his endless conquests, and the pursuit of power? The Red, destroying land and people under the hoofs of fire and brimstone? Or is it the Pale Horse, bringing only death, nothing more?

The hard truth is that it is all the above. It is also you and me. So many Americans have become futile in their thinking. See Romans 1:21. And please do not tell me you go to church, say grace, tithe, and pray when you go to bed. The corrupt leaders of the nations who foster all this cruelty, and who promote evil, who turn a blind eye to poverty and drugs, tolerate crime, and talk up war and violence do the same, as do those who support them.

Maybe you are horrified by this story or by the scenes of brutality currently being inflicted by the Russian military on the people of Ukraine. You may be asking, "What can I do about these things?" Truthfully, nothing. Even asking that question demonstrates ignorance and apathy. We have only one thing to do; we must turn to the Lord and seek His mercy and encourage everyone around us to do the same. And we should drop our phony "lifestyle" fixation and our materialism and devote ourselves in our hearts to helping one another in love, in genuine recognition that we are not morally superior to the addict in the street. We need to grow in compassion and humility; stop thinking we are something we are not. See Romans 12:3.

Yes, I am speaking harsh words. I am in a harsh mood. A young man I knew died. Others I care about are devastated. On our streets you can get enough Fentanyl to kill yourself for $2. And neither you, the police, the army, nor all the politicians of city, county, state, and federal government—the bureaucrats in neckties—or anyone else can do a thing about it. As my people round the way would say "It is what it is."

Hello! Are you awake? I will tell you a secret—all are dead who do not *know* God. Forget your almsgiving, your church attending, your lessons from Sunday school, unless you are a child. I am speaking to the grownups. No one can please God unless he *knows* God.

Our society, meaning the entirety of Western Civilization, has sold its soul to the devil. As we watch sports on TV, fill our bellies, drink alcohol, get pills for every minor ache and pain, play with our mobile devices, plan for cushy retirements, take cruises and vacations to the Gulf of Mexico, shop for clothes and gadgets and all the other selfish things[65] we do, we are doing one thing. We worship the flesh. The flesh wants; for that is what it does—all it does.

> "Those who live according to the flesh have their minds set on what the flesh desires; but those who live in accordance with the Spirit have their minds set on what the Spirit desires. The mind governed by the flesh is death; But the mind governed by the Spirit is life and peace; The mind governed by the flesh is hostile to God. It does not submit to God's law, nor can it do so. Those who are in the realm of the flesh cannot please God." Romans 8:5-8.

What is Paul telling us? If your heart is set on *anything* in this world to possess it, you play into the devil's hands. Also, greed, anger, and revenge—are all natural human motivations, but inevitably leading to death, and a death that is followed by hell. See, for example See Romans 12:19-20. As the Chinese proverb tells us, the one who sets out on a course of revenge should first dig two graves, one for the other and one for himself. Obviously, we all sin without meaning to do so. We are working on it.

Be advised: everything you think is yours is on loan, including the physical body. It all belongs to God. He will have it back in due time. Use it but take no pride in any of it. And "your" wife, "your" children, these are no more your possessions than the moon and the stars. You are expected to love and care for them, but you do not own them. And the One who brought you together will separate you from them when it is His good pleasure to do so.

Worldly thinking is the essence of sin. I hoard because whatever I am hoarding is more valuable to me than God. Some people hoarded toilet paper during the pandemic. How futile was their thinking?

God made us and put us here so that we, or some of us, would look for him, reach out to him and find him, and having done so, to devote ourselves to Him and serve our fellowman. See Acts 17: 24-28. This should

[65] Yes, the saved have freedom in that there are few rules. You can wear expensive symbols of privilege and fly to different places to have "fun," (that is, to please the flesh). But not everything is beneficial or helpful. See 1 Cor. 10:23-4.

be our daily, hourly goal. I know that we must put it aside momentarily at times to do other things. God knows that too. And that is OK. And there will be times when we just forget, or temptation is too overpowering. God is aware and He knows we can't be perfect. We ask for His forgiveness for the times we fail. And we will try again. Failing and trying again is a sure sign of real faith. See Romans 7:7-25. Keep this in mind so that when you do fail you do not lose heart; for that is the reason Paul wrote it.

The result over time though is a constant or almost constant awareness of His presence in everything. In my life, it is a running dialogue. For other people, it is just a feeling, knowing He is there.

What does all this have to do with a dead boy in a portable toilet? Everything! Unless you walk by faith, not by sight, you can do nothing. But the Holy Spirit can help you do many things. Things you "can't" do. Things you are afraid to do. It can make warriors out of the timid, leaders out of the tongue-tied, and strong people out of the emotionally crippled. In much the same way the Spirit will lead us to where we are supposed to be and show us things we are supposed to see. Most of all, it can take away our hearts of stone and give us hearts of flesh. That is, the ability to open our hearts and love people we used to cross the street to avoid, like priest and the Levite in the parable of the Good Samaritan. See Luke 10: 25-37.

What I am saying, what I am praying, and what I am begging is that each one of us open our hearts and come to Christ daily, follow the Holy Spirit, and that we have a revival of faith throughout America. We need to put aside our materialism and selfishness. These selfish tendencies lie behind the people who vociferously oppose building shelters in "their" neighborhoods or ask the police to break up homeless camps, or even arrest people just for being poor. Turning to Christ and opening one's eyes shows us the unnecessary cruelty of these actions. This is the only way, the only help, the only possibility of change that will really mean anything. This is the only way that we will reach a time when we no longer find boys locked in portable toilets, dead.

Yes, this death I'm speaking of was a tragedy. But in a greater sense our entire civilization right now is a tragedy. People do not know God, and because they do not know God they are doomed, and the civilization is doomed. If you want to save it; if you want to make anything better in the world, first you must let God save you and fix you, because no one can fix himself. But the good news is that it is not too late! We can still change, with God's help.

We should not be afraid of this. Those who are obedient will live. The commandment is to love God and love your neighbor as yourself. It isn't rocket science. Open your heart, let Him in and do this commandment. "Today, if you hear his voice do not harden your hearts." Hebrews 4:7.

Blessings and peace in the Holy Spirit and may the love of Christ be in you all.

Chapter Fifteen

THE TROPHY

Why was it such a big deal to Cain that Abel got the lion's share of praise, all smiles and affection, and he never seemed to be quite good enough? Why would this feeling be so strong as to lead him to murder his own brother?

Much of the misery in the world is caused by the overemphasis we place on achievement. Winning, success, climbing the ladder, celebrity worship, accumulation of money and things, attainment of rank and power, making a mark, etc., ad infinitum. Trophies. Diplomas. Awards. Letters after a person's name or titles that precede it. Honors and recognition. We even laud a person just for being a "billionaire;" "a star;" or "a success story." This is all pure nonsense. No one is a story of any kind, everyone is a spirit, and the only true success is measured in the heart by the One who will judge us all. Further, by putting anyone on a pedestal we do more harm to them than we know. That person is then faced with the temptation of believing it, and of the idolatry of self; while we who idolize them are guilty of the same sin. And all of it leads to death of the spirit. Isn't this also the reason so many such "idols" become drunkards, addicts, or suicides? I avoid naming people in my writing, but you could tick off the list in your own mind of really famous people who have had these problems and worse.

Taking all the success and achievement talk too seriously leads to self-comparison and depression. Kids raised in middle-class America are raised to believe in achievement, competition, and comparison.[66] And, unfortunately, they are often overwhelmed by the idolatry of achievement. Make the team, make the grade, win the championship, get the scholarship. Be the star, the valedictorian, number one. But sadly, only one can be the number one; no one else can. And it is bad both for the number one and for everyone else as well. No one will always be number one.

Keep in mind that shame, the fear that one is not all he or she or ze[67] should be, the negative self-perception triggered by the trick the devil played on Eve, is also used as a prybar to steal the spirit, and make people feel less-than all the time. The driving motor that tells us we cannot live up to the example of our parents, peers, or heroes, and that if we do not, then we are pathetic "losers," and a waste of life. This is always a lie straight from the forked tongue of the serpent in the Garden and is the very thing that stops so many from being all we could be, living fully today according to God's plan, and rejoicing in it. Much of our acquisitiveness is driven by the sense of shame. We must get our kids into private school. We must have a house that is as nice as those of our friends and associates. We must dress a certain way. We must have "standards."

And for some, that includes being "number one," first in class, captain of the football team, of the cheerleaders, or whatever Mom or Dad did. And if we fail that, the shame is too much to bear and we might as well kill ourselves, and if we can't even do that, we get drunk or stoned, or "drop out" and go where people appreciate us. Even if that means prostitution or jail. I see it all the time out here in Realville.

When there comes a day that being number one will not avail, when you get cancer, when you have everything taken away in the pandemic, when your children die, what good is it to be number one? Or, when you are finally caught by age and decrepitude, and all you can do is sit in a bar with your friends and swap stories of "glory days," what do you really

---

66 I'm not forgetting that there are also children of poverty to be concerned with, who have never known any success, achievement, awards, or recognition for accomplishment. And I frequently give the young men "the talk" wherein I encourage them and tell them they can become something more than a fifty-year-old street person.

67 Some people may gasp and say I am not being Biblical, etc. Such people are driven by fear and doubt. I am not condoning sexual immorality of any kind, but if we recognize we are all sinners, then there is hope. Jesus can save the addict, the drinker, the thief, the preacher's adulterous wife and the person of gender difference. And while they try to not sin, just like Paul in Romans chapter seven, we all struggle with sin. So, I am being intellectually honest including everyone in the call, knowing that for God all things are possible. If this frightens anyone, such could be a fruitful subject to pray on for them. Let the one without sin cast the first stone.

have? Only to wash away your sadness with alcohol. I know a lot of people like this; polishing their bar stool at their favorite spot, wasting days that should be filled with excitement and the joy of living in the Lord, bragging about whatever they did forty or fifty years ago.

And those who are not number one will always think they are second-best, or that no matter how hard they try, they never seem to be good enough or they never seem to "get anywhere."

Isn't it sad? And people become bitter and cynical and disappointed. They don't understand what is wrong with them. Why can't they be number one? And if they used to be number one, they are depressed because now someone else is number one.

All these false ideas of course lead to depression, self-destructive behavior, dependency on alcohol or drugs, prescribed or not prescribed, or just malaise, a state of lack of motivation and disengagement. And all are based on incorrect thinking and the idolatry of achievement and success; and the false premise that "I"—the worldly self—is what is important. Or alternatively that other people and their ideas are important. That is, how they evaluate "me;" or how I think they might evaluate "me."

And people spend tons of money and precious time *trying* to fix themselves; trying to improve their game, trying to compensate for whatever they think they lack, trying to get out of the feeling that life is passing them by, that they have wasted it, that they aren't good enough for the expectations of others. There are self-help books, online courses, motivational speakers, yoga classes, weight loss, cosmetic surgery; the list is endless. All for people who feel they are not good enough as they are.

The cost of all this is tremendous, because by spending their whole lives trying to fix these non-existent problems, or even creating new ones like alcoholism, people miss the chance to fully live today. They pour their life's energy, time, and money down a rabbit hole, when instead they could be living an engaged, exciting life full of meaning and purpose every day, serving God and others.

But "There remains then a Sabbath rest for the people of God" See Hebrews 4:9. For those who come to Him we have a Great High Priest who intercedes for us, and He already knows your heart; there is nothing that can stop you. See Hebrews 4:14-16. Today if you hear the call (if you are still reading this, you *are* hearing the call), please, do not harden your heart.

You have no need to be number one or any other number. Life is not about worldly success or achievement. It is well to learn a trade, or a profession and to do well in it, to try hard. To serve the people of this world the best you can. And to save something so that you do not become a burden to others in your old age, and so that you have something to share with the poor. There is nothing wrong with any of that. What is wrong is to elevate in one's mind the importance of achievement or accumulation, or the lack of them. To "glorify" these things—meaning to elevate or "worship" something other than God—is a form of *idolatry*. All human beings are on the same level. No one should think of anyone living or dead as special, except for Jesus Christ.

We are merely God's servants. It is more important to serve, to sacrifice, to speak the truth, to be humble, and to love others with a true heart. What enables you to be like this is *believing in* Jesus and recognizing who He is and what He died for. And there is a life, a better life, available to us now. Living with eyes open, breathing fresh air we can live unbound from chains of anxiety and depression. As servants, we do not need to win anything. God wins, we just have to serve. And as a reward, when we serve well, we will feel the Holy Spirit moving through us, and we will feel assured that God is with us even if we die.

Following the Holy Spirit is a chance to get outside of the "box." As Jesus pointed out, the Spirit is not contained. See John 3:8. The problem with many people is that they do not want to consider anything outside the box. They are comfortable inside the box, so why would they want to think about what is outside the box? And this is true of Christians as much as anyone. They smile in church and cry into their pillows at night about their situations, their broken hearts, their seeming failures, and their disappointments. They have all the same problems as others, but shame is increased by the belief that they are supposed to be better. They sit in a sanctuary full of Christians every Sunday and no one feels comfortable with discussing their divorce, their mistakes, their fears. Jesus Christ did not set us free so we could just imprison ourselves in another box! See Galatians 5:1.

Nicodemus, a Pharisee came to see Jesus at night (a fact which tells you a lot if you think about it) and was informed that he could see the Kingdom of

God, but first he must be born again. Unfortunately, this was hard to understand for Nicodemus, who was a man of learning, but stuck inside the box. He was Israel's teacher, and obviously Judaism wasn't giving him the peace and joy he needed; and it wasn't providing the answer to the life issues he dealt with, whatever those were. Thus, he sought out Jesus at night, hoping for something more. We also can seek out Jesus at night in our beds, in our houses, or in a cell. But poor Nicodemus missed it because he was stuck inside the box.

The problem with the box is that once we are inside, we can't see what is outside. This is what happened to Eve when she and Adam were tricked into the sin of worldly blindness and self-consciousness by Satan.

Existentialists a hundred years ago concluded that life is "absurd." We are born, we grow up, we toil, we reproduce, we die. No God, meaningless suffering, final death. The fate of man without God. See also Ecclesiastes in the Bible, who drew the same conclusion thousands of years ago, but found restoration in faith.[68]

And in this state of mind people worry about the future and devote energy to regrets about the past. We cannot change the past, nor can we predict the future. These things just rob us of *today*. But to know God and his Son, Jesus, opens the eyes so that we can stop worrying about the past, for we are forgiven. We can stop worrying about the future; we are not condemned. See John 5:24. We can stop thinking about not getting anywhere, since we are where God has put us. We can stop worrying about achievement and focus on doing God's work. And the rewards of that are plentiful, many times what we give.

> "Jesus heard that they had thrown [the man born blind] out and when he had found him, he said, 'Do you believe in the Son of Man?' 'Who is he, sir?' the man asked. Tell me so that I may believe in him.' Jesus said, 'You have now seen him; in fact, he is the one speaking with you.' Then the man said, 'Lord, I believe,' and he worshipped him." John 9:30-38.

This is the real trophy, the prize, the cornerstone the worldly men rejected. And remember, the Kingdom of God is about righteousness, *joy*, and peace in the Holy Spirit! See Romans 14:17. So be happy!

[68] Believed to have been written by Soloman.

Chapter Sixteen

A Stronger Heart

In Matthew 26, Jesus had been praying in the garden at Gethsemane.

> "Then he came to the disciples and found them sleeping; and he said to Peter, 'So, you could not stay awake with me one hour? Stay awake and pray that you may not come into the time of trial; the spirit indeed is willing, but the flesh is weak'." Matthew 26:40-42.

Where did these pandemic years go? I am completely tired of wearing face masks. But, yesterday, the shelter where I volunteer closed for the day because several people got Covid. "They" (government? doctors?) say it's still a threat. The news says people are afraid of supply chain shortages. Our weak and corrupt leaders have pursued policies that have left us dependent on China and other far away countries for everything from electronics to toilet paper. And people are afraid! Many people are suffering, gas is expensive, rent is unaffordable, and so is food. Gone are the seven years of plenty, it seems; now come the seven years of sorrow. It snuck up on us like a thief in the night.

What drove the toilet paper panic of 2020, when every shelf was empty, and you couldn't even buy it on Amazon? It was a blind panic. Now a new thing is happening, spreading, and increasing poverty. A combination of unfortunate government policies, combined with the pandemic, and a global slowdown resulting in widespread suffering and loss of material well-being are the new reality.

After Jesus spoke to a woman at the well of Jacob in John 4, his disciples came and asked if he were hungry, remember?

> "Jesus said, 'I have food to eat that you do not know about.' The disciples said to one another, 'Surely no one has brought him something to eat.' Jesus said to them: 'My food is to do the will of him who sent me and to complete his work. Do you not say four months more and then comes the harvest? But I tell you look around you and see how the fields are ripe for harvesting. The reaper is already receiving wages and gathering fruit for eternal life, so that the Sower and the reaper may rejoice together'." John 4:32-35.

Jesus saw with clarity things as they really are and knew who we are and why we are here. And he shared this human existence with us so that we can share life and the Spirit with Him. I didn't know him, although he was my brother and yet, He died for me. But he laid down his life and picked it back up again. In my darkest hour he came to me and took all my negatives and nailed them to the cross and gave me of his infinite Spirit a small drop, which is the most amazing experience anyone can have in this life. The smallest drop of what He has, and you will never be the same.

One of the things He has given me is the certainty that there is another life, not off in space somewhere with pearly gates, or floating on a cloud, but existing all around and within us, which is the spiritual realm. Further, our fundamental nature is not a being of clay with something called a soul attached to it, a seldom used appendage. No! We are spirits of light! God, YHWH, Elohim has loaned us this body, this vehicle—avatar if you will—for His purposes, His plan, each to play our part in it. We are to do His work. At the same time, carrying out His tasks; suffering and sacrificing in this flesh grows us and perfects us as spirits, to be fit to be in His presence. Through suffering, we learn perseverance and through sacrifice we learn humility. See, Romans 5:3-5. Through helping others, we learn love. No person who does not develop these qualities is fit to enter God's kingdom.

I've had a lot of catching up to do the last few years. But He gave me a second chance.

One challenge about this flesh existence is the fact that the flesh-body does one thing from birth to the grave: it wants. We must feed it, water it, avoid danger, and all the necessary things of life. And God, who made it and loaned it to us, arranged our brain chemistry to help. Dopamine, oxytocin, and adrenaline all serve this purpose. They are the "feel good" chemistry of the brain.

Unfortunately, these chemicals are also stimulated by all the unwholesome activities we label sin. And they are the biological reason we become slaves to sin. The devil has used the inner chemistry of the flesh to play all sorts of dirty tricks with us—addiction to drugs, to sex, pornography, and to our own creations like cell phones, money, and TV. He has used it to get us to worship the idolatries of success, money, self-image, and something we call our "lifestyle," all of which are fruitless. And even worldly wisdom, as Paul discusses in 1 Corinthians, chapter 1, is a blind alley. These are all dead ends, all chaff in the wind. Read Ecclesiastes; he spelled it out in simple straightforward language. Furthermore, these cravings of the body and the mind are traps, things that entice people out into the spiritual desert and abandon them there. Jesus passed that test; can you?

Yeshua, the man, had to eat, but was not a slave to food. See Matthew 4:4. Instead, being fully aware of the shortness of His time, and always seeing in the spirit, He was able to do without worldly comforts. He lived homeless, he wore cheap clothes, he appeared little more than a beggar, but he had something about him that drew people to him. He walked comfortably among the poor, and even lepers and outcasts; yet the rich came to Him and invited him into their homes. All the barriers were transcended in Him. But you don't have to be someone special to be like this. Every Christian should work on this. You just must learn to see the spirit in people. My eyes were opened like the man born blind. I do hate "down time" when I cannot be in my own calling. But my heart is full, and my spirit is flying. Everyone's calling is different, and people's experiences are different, but we can all serve in some capacity.[69]

If we look at Hebrews 2:10-18, we see that Jesus was made a little lower than the angels so that He could suffer as we suffer, and He was perfected through suffering, and we are perfected through suffering. He experienced the death of the flesh out of His vast compassion because we experience the death of the flesh. And because of these joint experiences we share with Him, He is not ashamed to call us His brothers and sisters. And If His brothers and sisters, we are also joint heirs with Him! See Galatians 4:6-7. That is, we are heirs to eternal life in His glorious kingdom, drinking forever from the River of Life.

So, because his compassion and his spirit were so great, and He gave so much, can we give of our limited stock less than whatever we have? As we see our brother Jesus nailed to the wood, do we offer nothing in our hearts? I say we are blessed if we suffer and die for him, whatever that entails. It took cancer for me to even see him. Always trying with my eyes of flesh, and my little logical brain, trying to figure it out. And wham! My world turned upside down. All I could do was to cry weakly, "Jesus! Help me." And he answered, "I thought you'd never ask." You see, He had been waiting all my life for the moment I would be able to break through all the preconceived ideas and logic and educated thought to grasp the truth and realize that there is more, much more to this existence than I ever dreamed was possible. There is no chasm between a wealthy lawyer and a homeless addict. Because the constructs we see in the worldly eye are a sham! Since then, my life has been a nonstop adventure. Every day has been a lifetime, every activity a thrill. After five years I testify that this is a lasting change in my life.

You know it is hard to see for several reasons. My eyes were veiled until I met him. Read 2 Corinthians 3:14-16. But the Holy Spirit opened the Bible for me, and it is as clear as a perfect October sky. God, the almighty force that moved the universe of space, time, and matter into existence, gave us reason and free will and asked us to come to him by our own choice, knowing many or even most will not. So, he always planned to send his son as a shepherd and high priest to lead us. If you doubt that

[69] Romans 12:6-8; 1 Corinthians 12:7-11. This is my personal experience; we are not going to be alike. It's an example of what it could be like based on my life.

look at Genesis 14:17-20; 22:1-19; see also Acts 17:24-27; Ephesians 1:3-12. All the way back in Genesis, God revealed his promise, the sacrifice of his son, and blessings to all mankind. This was always the plan, and God's plans are always perfect.

In Hebrews 7:1-10, the author explains about Melchizedek, King of Salem, who appears in Genesis 14:17-20, and compares him to Christ, and contrasts him with the Levitical priesthood. God anointed Jesus to be the Great High Priest forever, who comes to those who are ready and who submit to Him. He alone was given the power to intercede for us with God, because of the sacrifice of His own blood, His physical existence, on our behalf. Why does this matter to you and me? The answer is that, when you study the religious practice of the Hebrews of old, it was all built around the system of feasts and sacrifices, and the Levitical priesthood making peace with God for our blindness and errors. But only the High Priest could mediate between the people and God. He could only enter the Most Holy Place—where the Ark of the Covenant was kept, where God heard pleas and gave responses—once a year on the Day of Atonement, and only with blood for his own sins and the sins of the people. This was because the human High Priest was as weak and fallible as everyone else. Further, the ritual washings and cleansings, and the blood sacrifices were only a patch or an *external* remedy and didn't clear the consciences of those who had gone seriously wrong. See Hebrews 9:13-14. By the way, that's everybody. See Romans 3. Sorry. We are sinners. We are trying to do better, but we all have "junk in the trunk."

We live in a world where the religion of materialism has taken over. Schools teach that the physical world is all there is. They try to say that if you believe in God, you must deny science. This is not true, but that is another discussion.

Commercialism, entertainment, and sensuality are constantly preached to us by advertising and the internet and even through friends and family. Do you know people who go to church, but put more life and passion into fantasy football than they do into Jesus Christ and his mission? Or people who are more obsessed with their own physical appearances and "lifestyles" than they are with doing God's work on earth? These seem innocuous enough in themselves. But there is a problem.

What you focus on most of the time becomes the center of your world. And when the storm of life comes with wind and fire and lightning, the center must hold. If the center is yourself, there will come a time of testing when you cannot save yourself, and you will have nothing to hold onto, because the death of the flesh is part of the storm, for everyone. If the center is other people, you will be bitterly disappointed because people are fallible, fickle, and weak; they break your heart, leave, abandon, betray and "ghost" you, no matter how strong and true they appear. You can never be sure of them because they cannot even be sure of themselves. And of course, they die. Furthermore, looks fade, the body disintegrates, money and fortunes are lost when the pandemic hits. Property and possessions are left behind in physical death. Read Ecclesiastes chapters 1 and 2. It is all worthless, fruitless, pointless. Camus, the existentialist writer, recognized this and, being an atheist, and rebelling at the "unexplained" fact of suffering, particularly of infants and other innocents, that (as he saw it) would not be allowed by a "just God," he posited that the only question left is whether to commit suicide.[70] If there were no such thing as a just God, and there is no eternity for us, the question hangs over us, "What is there to live for?"

I think Camus must have been another "glass-half-empty" person like Cain. If someone asks for water and a waiter brings them a glass exactly half full of perfect clear water, some people will perceive the glass as half full and drink it; others will perceive it as half empty and complain. I'm presuming they aren't charging for the water by the ounce or by the cup. It's a matter of orientation, what one expects in life. But it is also a sign of materialism, a mind focused on the flesh, which *always* wants more. And without God we are necessarily focused on the flesh, as Paul says in Romans 8:5-8, the mind focused on the sinful nature (material world) is death, but the mind focused on the Spirit is life and peace.

Therefore, if the knowledge of the reality beyond the physical world is clearly in focus in your mind and you see it, then the deeper reality of this

[70] What is justice? If we are completely honest, none of us deserves Heaven, based on merit. Eternal life is a gift, paid for with the blood of Christ. And the suffering of the flesh is often necessary to get us there, to get rid of our pride, to bring us broken to the foot of the cross. This is what it took for me. I know my worst physical sufferings are still ahead, and all I ask is strength and courage to accept them and to do His will. All of this is for my benefit, given by a merciful God.

existence also comes into focus. God is the center, the first and the last, the reason for everything. He is the giver of both worlds and not like we are used to with people or government, giving with one hand while snatching back with the other. In Jesus the answer is always "yes." See 2 Corinthians 1:19.

The physical body was taken from the earth and with the earth it must stay. The potter digs clay from the riverbank and forms it and fires it to use as a vessel for water, wine, oil etc. In the end, it is usually just pieces tossed in the rubbish and broken down by the elements. But the spirit is the eternal part. See 2 Corinthians 4:7. We don't throw out a vessel with the juice still in it. Our father loaned us this body so we can fulfill His purposes. It is meant to be seen as a tool. Useful, but not be-all or end-all. Just as we should not worship bits of stone and wood we make with our hands; we should not regard any physical object as more than it is, including our physical body. See Romans 12:3.

We also construct mental ideas of the past, the future, our place in the world. What do they mean? Nothing! This is one lesson the homeless teach. All the things you think you have you really do not have. You imagine that they are something they are not. This gives rise to a lot of anxiety, fears about the future, what will happen, or could happen. I could get Covid, have a heart attack, fall climbing, get shot going into a "bad" area doing my work for outreach, or die from these cancers I have. I can picture myself lying in bed waiting for death with a hospice nurse attending me. Bah! Humbug! If I focus an extra second of my life thinking about this idea that second is wasted, and I don't have seconds to spare. I am living on purpose, doing on purpose. The future will take care of itself. The moment is eternal. No matter what time it is, it is always now.

Your worldly job could be as an attorney or the President. You may think that defines you, but it does not. A man may think he is a drunk, an addict or an ex-convict. He is not that either! This is all false. You and I are not merely these mental constructs, but rather we are beings of light and spirit who have been gifted the use of this flesh for a purpose. By seeing this spiritual truth clearly, our world is turned upside down from the perspective of those trapped in the limited vision of only the material that is unable to discern matters of the Spirit. See 1 Corinthians 2:10-16.

Therefore, I describe a passionate life as waking up in the morning and feeling you can't wait to get to your Godly calling or cannot wait to get together with your brothers and sisters to join hands in praise. Passion is when it's 4:00 a.m. and you can't wait to get up to your Bible and revel in its glory! Compassion is when you stop in traffic to help a homeless person by the side of the road or use your vacation time for Godly work like helping the flood victims in eastern Kentucky because you feel a call.

Someone said we should shut up about Jesus in polite company. I cannot. Someone says it's too risky to go down on the riverbank at night. Risky to what? Someone says. The devil pushes back when you are passionate about Christ, and you suffer all sorts of things for him. Sometimes you suffer rejection, humiliation, shaming, and derision. See Matthew 5:10-12. Sometimes people die for him. This is a growing problem. There are about 100,000 annually who are martyred for this faith, refusing to relinquish His blessing, even at gunpoint. Passion for Him and for people and for life, in this eternal moment, led by the Holy Spirit means it is all an adventure, it all has meaning. Whatever day it is, it is always today; whatever time it is, it is always now. Now never ends, and we live in this moment perpetually serving the Master of the universe and the King of the eternal Spirit.

The day before his assassination, Martin Luther King said he was happy. Reading his speech, it is clear he expected something to happen. Doctor King spoke of his life, discussing all the things that had happened in his life since he had been stabbed at an event some ten years before and nearly died. But he was aware that he was here for a purpose, and even though he might not be here much longer he was *happy* to be doing God's work. Such was his passion. He was in the moment, feeling the Spirit.

My own challenges are different. Statistically, I have already lived past the expected time for my cancer, and I now have a second form of cancer, so I don't know whether they or something else will finally set me free. But the time grows shorter. God keeps me here for His purpose. I served meals in the homeless shelter through the worst of the pandemic and at that time there were no shots or proven treatments. Other friends died, but by God's grace there was no Covid 19 in the shelter.[71] God, in His mercy

[71] It is somewhat amazing to me because we had fifty people sleeping in two open dormitories and things like social distancing and mask rules were impossible to enforce. People died in the nursing homes, but as far as I can tell, Covid had very little effect on the homeless population, nationally.

placed His hand over us. It's the only explanation I can conceive of. He is sovereign over all things. I may have already done what He wanted, or there might be more, but this I know: I am happy to be doing His work today. I am determined, even when the flesh is weak, to continue to serve until I physically die. Doing His will sustains me. I feel that the living water flows through me. See John 7:38. Passion for my Lord who gave so much, denying Himself, drives me in my heart.

This is the transformation that *begins* with belief and salvation when we come to Him; but it grows over time through service and obedience and testing. We must be mentally determined to finish the race no matter what. When adversity, danger or painful life experiences come, we gradually teach ourselves to see them as tests, given by our merciful God to grow our spirits and to weigh our spiritual progress. If we maintain our passion for the Lord and our compassion for others through these tests, we grow our power in the Holy Spirit.

> "And we, who with unveiled faces all reflect the Lord's glory, are being transformed into His likeness with ever-increasing glory, which comes from the Lord, who is the Spirit." 2 Cor. 3:18.

And so long as I feel that passion, by God's grace, I can always go a little farther. I pray that God keeps me focused and determined so that nothing stops me until my race is completed here. I pray He supplements my strength and courage and determination to continue. I pray that even when I make mistakes, sin without intending to sin, hurting people without intending to hurt them, that He leads me past it and keeps me going and does not let me get stuck with sorrow and worry about it. I pray I can be kinder and more gracious to everyone. I pray to be generous, giving, thoughtful and selfless, even right up to my dying. It is the constant giving, the focus on Him, and on people I serve that takes my attention away from everything negative that I could dwell on. Therefore, instead of fear and sorrow, I feel joy and excitement daily, and I can live a beautiful life here and now.

Think of this: a beautiful sunny day, a crystalline blue sky, people going to-and-fro, but not hurrying, enjoying the beauty of it all, stopping and helping one another, calling out in the street to acquaintances, stopping and chatting. And if one has an experience worth sharing, he or she feels comfortable sharing, or if anyone is sad, he or she can share his or her sadness without shame, confess without guilt. And everyone understands, no one puts on false smiles, nothing pierces the inner joy of the Spirit, all are at peace. No one crosses the street to avoid anyone. Everyone shares, not for guilt, but as naturally as the children in the old mulberry tree all those years ago on that other sunny perfect day.

Each of us can be more like this, each of us can share Jesus's love, each of us can be blessed in the God who made us, not rushed, not afraid. All we would need to do is to let go and let Him in, surrender our pride, give up our trophies, forego lifestyle, end the competition to be number one. But it cannot be done by some government, it must come from the heart.

> "I will put my law in their minds and write it on their hearts. I will be their God and they will be my people. No longer will they teach their neighbor or say to one another 'know the Lord,' because they will all know me, from the least of them to the greatest,
>
> declares the Lord.
>
> For I will forgive their wickedness and remember their sins no more." Jer. 31:33-34.

God will write on everyone's heart the love of Himself and of other people and give us the vision to know Him, as we know our families, not just what people say about him, but by direct experience of His presence. And the vision that comes with that is to see the spirit in other people, so that each of them appears to us as a spiritual presence. And the love of Christ is a beating heart within us.

The truth is that this is not going to happen to the whole world until the end of time, when God remakes the world in His image. Sad as that is, all we can do is turn it over to the Lord for ourselves. But in doing so we can be blessed by love and peace and joy in the Holy Spirit right now. And we can stop and help a street person, we can lend a shoulder to cry on to those who suffer, even strangers, we can listen to the stories they tell, we can see the yearnings of their spirits, share the pangs in their hearts, the sorrows in their eyes. We needn't give them false smiles; they would be better served with tears. Just listen and believe them and sometimes share the story of Jesus with those who are open. And never give up. That is the stronger heart. A Jesus heart, beating steadily in the eternal moment. Being alive in every way today, led and living in the Spirit. So, my prayer for each of you is that somewhere as you have read this book, something has rung true for you, something has woken up and come alive; if you have not already given yourself over to the Lord, that a mustard seed has been planted, which will eventually grow and blossom and bear fruit. I pray that when the winds and tides of life rip away all you thought you had, you will remember the mulberry tree and that you can regain that joyful spirit with the Lord's help, and that all that is necessary is simply to humble yourself with a true heart in all your brokenness, let go of the ashes of what you thought you had, and give yourself to Him who gave Himself for you. Peace and blessings.

> *"With joy you will draw water from the wells of my salvation."*
> Isaiah 12:3

Postscript

This book is intended to challenge people. It is intended to challenge Christians to live a more spiritual life; that is, to really work on it, through daily meditation, prayer, and study. It is intended to inspire Christians to put their faith into action in their calling, in service to mankind. You will not find this passion and spirit inside "the box."[72] You have to be willing to do new things, open to hearing Him call, and willing to answer.

---

[72] As I see it, the box is composed of the things we learn as children in Sunday School, plus, official church doctrine, customs of Western Civilization, and compromises that are made between the demands of the world and the call of Jesus Christ. As I read the Lord's words to the churches in Revelation, I fear every word is a problem for Twenty-First Century Christians, especially in America. I fear we tend to deceive ourselves like the Laodiceans, thinking we are all we should be, but spiritually we are still drifting farther from the spiritual and selfless examples set by Jesus and Paul. And we cannot see it because we are afraid to peek outside the box. Some even rationalize that our prosperity is a reward for virtue. This is exactly what the Laodiceans thought. Others think following an established pattern will "get you into heaven." Read the first chapter of the book of Isaiah. You have to get out of the box, and once you do, it would be wise to burn the box.

It is also intended to challenge all the religious institutions to focus less on money and trust God to provide. To care less about buildings and objects and to be more concerned with developing a close community among their members. It is intended to inspire those who are not already prioritizing this to greater humanitarian service.

It is intended to challenge doctrines and dogmas and rituals and customs, so that we are not trapped by them like the Pharisees of Jesus day. Reading Isaiah, it is clear that, while these things have a purpose, they are not essential to God's plan, and many are not even Biblical. What the Bible calls for is a spiritual connection with our Creator through Jesus Christ and living in awareness of the Holy Spirit.

It is intended to challenge teachers and ministers to teach and exhort people to understand the place of suffering and how to use the inevitable suffering in this life as an opportunity for growth. That is, not to wait until someone gets cancer, but to talk about these things openly and share experiences of real life on an ongoing basis and encourage everyone to do the same; to demonstrate living and growing in the spirit.

It is intended to show people the destructiveness of all forms of materialism, including the association of Christmas presents and candy and the custom of dressing themselves in finery for worship. The subtle forms of materialism that people think are innocuous are not. And we should not be teaching kids to expect toys and presents and candy; rather we should encourage gratitude and sharing.

Communities are formed by sharing real feelings, real experiences. Bible communities use scripture to help people work through the hard parts. Forced smiles, special "church clothes," too-tight handshakes, insincere "sorrys," and constant demands for cash diminish and obscure the real message of Christ. Teaching about reality should begin from childhood. Kids will not stay with something they perceive as fake. In my opinion, no Santa Claus, Christmas trees, presents, candy or other such materialist nonsense should be in church. Easter egg hunts and chocolate rabbits may seem "nice" but really these are "feel good" moments for grandparents and are subtle enticements from the one who tempted Eve. Most often the devil comes to us attractively packaged and robs us and leaves us desolate long before we realize what has happened.

If this seems too harsh, and austere, and "not fun" then tell me where in the life of Jesus and Paul and the apostles does the Bible talk about fun? *Fun is the act of in some way pleasing the flesh.* And while I do not regard this as "a sin" or reason to feel guilt, I definitely want to caution people that there is a danger in that people become addicted to those feel-good chemicals in the brain and can become "slaves" to them as Paul says. A "fun lifestyle" tends to supplant the rightful place of Jesus Christ in one's life.

Generosity of spirit should be a year-round characteristic of Christians, as should forgiveness, tolerance, kindness, simplicity, and love of people. "Success" and being "number one" are false values. Self-sacrifice should be valued above worldly gain and competition. We should teach our children humility by example.

I believe these are the values of the Bible. These are the values of Jesus Christ set forth in Matthew 5. This does not mean to not allow children to play; play is a learning and growing experience. But, if they are on a computer playing "Diablo" or "Grand Theft Auto" or many other commercially successful games, what are they learning?

I believe the organized church needs reform, and Christians should educate themselves through independent Bible study and demand that their churches be Biblical in every way they can. Many of the cultural trappings added to the church in the Middle Ages should be dropped as non-Biblical. Organizations are afraid attendance will drop and collections will suffer. In my opinion, children growing up with a deeper sense of reality in the church and seeing congruence in their parents' lives are more likely to become religious themselves and to avoid the devil's traps of materialism, sex, and drugs.

I want to be clear about this point: saying these things, *I am not talking about sin as breaking some rule and then feeling guilty about it.* Sin is worldly desire, the cravings of the natural self, the body, and the mind, for the things of the world. The idea is not to create guilt or shame, but to guide people into spirituality, and away from materialism. Jesus died to abolish guilt and shame. We are as God made us; we are where He put us. There is nothing inherently wrong with us. We simply need to be focused on the right things and our lives can be joyful and positive right now, and the wellspring of joy will overflow into eternity with our God. This is what YHWH always intended for us. But He wants us to reach out for Him voluntarily, and to worship Him in our hearts. That is what this life is all about.

If your children do not see reality in this faith, they will not stay with it. If you talk about church, but football or money is what you demonstrate is more important, that is what they will learn.

Remember also, stupid arguments about words, debatable matters, rules, and obscure doctrines only harm those who are young in faith. See 2 Tim. 2:23. People on social media want to draw you into these fruitless arguments so that they can feel superior. Ignore them.

So, walk in the spirit, serve God first and then other people. Do these with a glad heart and demonstrate joy and inner peace. Do not value anything in this world very highly. In trying times, learn to realize that you are being tested and turn to God, read the Bible, and do not panic. Do not be like those who value material things too highly.

Lastly, remember, these changes take a lifetime. You cannot be perfect. If you are walking the walk you will fail at times. Expect this and pick yourself up and keep walking. Try, fail, try again. This is Christianity in action. We are only human beings. Stay humble.

Lastly, I always conclude with this: we paid nothing for the opportunity to experience life in the flesh. It was given to us as a gift. We did nothing to deserve salvation through Jesus' blood on the cross that saves us from our mistakes and wrong turns. Yet it is ours for the asking. A gift. Everything that matters is a gift. And we are alive today. Today is the day the Lord has made. Rejoice and be happy in it.

With love,
Joe

www.ingramcontent.com/pod-product-compliance
Ingram Content Group UK Ltd.
Pitfield, Milton Keynes, MK11 3LW, UK
UKHW022018190726
13853UKWH00005B/1989

9 798330 411177